Teaching Mentally Handicapped Children

A Handbook of Practical Activities

Barbara Brooks

Ward Lock Educational

ISBN 0 7062 3721 8 hardback
   0 7062 3634 3 paperback

First published 1978

Set in 11 on 12 point Bembo
by Computacomp (UK) Limited, Fort William
and printed by The Whitefriars Press Ltd.,
London and Tonbridge
for Ward Lock Educational
116 Baker Street, London W1M 2BB
A member of the Pentos Group
Made in Great Britain

Contents

Photographs taken by W. Rhodes Marriott, A.I.I.P., A.R.P.S. at Margaret Whitehead School, Salford, with kind permission of the Headteacher, Mrs Joan Tomkinson.

Acknowledgments

I am especially grateful to Mrs Joan Tomkinson, Headteacher, Margaret Whitehead School, Salford, for helping me and giving me the opportunity to develop my own ideas for different age groups within the school, and for her encouraging suggestions during the initial stages of this book. I would like to thank, too, all the teaching staff of that school for their lively and creative art work, which gave me the idea of compiling a book.

In particular I would like to thank Mrs Barbara Kola for her frequent help, advice and suggestions. Thanks also to Shirley Haslam, Anne Davies and Helen Myers whose notes gave me ideas for additional material.

I would like to extend a special thank-you to Mrs Mildred Stevens, M.Ed., who was my tutor on the N.A.M.H. (now MIND) course at Manchester. It was she who initiated the varied curriculum which is essential for teaching the mentally handicapped, and this provided a solid foundation for my teaching and inspired this book. Due credit must also go to the other tutors on the 1968–70 course; in particular I would like to thank Mrs Pat Simpson (Art), Mrs Thorley (Movement) and Mrs McKay (Cookery).

I am indebted to Mrs Marion Nicholls for her accurate and speedy typing, and to Mrs Christine Ramsay who proved a worthy substitute when Mrs Nicholls was away.

I would also like to thank most sincerely my parents, who gave me endless advice and encouragement throughout the compiling of this book and for their continuing help and guidance.

Finally, I shall always be grateful to my husband, first for drawing the original diagrams and later for helping me with the proofs, but mostly for his good humour and understanding, without which this book would never have been completed.

Part 1

General Information

1 Introduction

Successfully teaching a mentally handicapped child to lead a more normal life can be a most useful and rewarding experience. This handbook of ideas has been designed specifically to help teachers create a curriculum to stimulate each child, improving both his behaviour and his intellectual ability. The teacher will naturally develop his or her own method of communicating these ideas so the suggestions should only be regarded as a basis from which different activities could grow and develop fully. The teacher is expected to have a more professional approach to the mentally handicapped now that the school is run by the Education Committee instead of the Health Department and each child has, at last, been recognized as 'educable'. Yet, despite this fact, there is no specific curriculum laid down for Educationally Sub-Normal, severe Schools to follow and there are no examinations for the child to strive for. Therefore the teachers have few guidelines, except basic play, pre-number and pre-reading exercises. Doubtless these have their values but they can also be limiting, as each child requires repetitive teaching whilst making comparatively slow progress. Consequently, his teacher is forever searching for fresh material to help her teach the same subject or skill in a different fashion.

There are parents too who limit their handicapped child by being overprotective towards him, thus depriving him of many normal experiences. Therefore additional aims of teachers involve integrating the child socially. By virtue of his disability, the child draws attention to himself, and comments from the general public upon his behaviour can be either damaging or rewarding.

People who are not involved with a handicapped child may be surprised at the way he can learn to respond to discipline: not, of course, harsh corporal punishment which the word may suggest but by encouragement, example and by the determination of the teacher to be consistent. For instance, if a normal three year old is seen stamping his feet and having a little tantrum, people will chuckle and make a light-hearted comment. If, however, a sixteen year old (who may have a *mental* age of three) is seen behaving in the same manner, he will lose all his dignity and people will turn away, believing him to be 'mental'. It is, therefore, up to the teacher — where possible in conjunction with the parents — to demand a high standard from the child. She should *expect* him to behave in a superior manner so that he will learn how to behave more normally. Good manners are particularly important at the dinner table and it can be exhausting trying to teach the child from a deprived area when there are no standards set at home. Perseverance and the vigilant care taken by the teacher to maintain her own standards should help the child imitate and learn. Eventually, it is hoped that he may be taken into a café by his parents or teacher who will feel proud of his good manners, polite behaviour and, hopefully, the public may not even notice he is 'different'.

If it is accepted that each child in the ESNs (Educationally Sub-Normal, severe) school can be disciplined, then it follows that with practice and well-organized activities he can be taught and educated in many varied skills.

It is also necessary to *teach* the children with additional handicaps in the Special Care Unit, who can be so easily forgotten or dismissed as being totally unresponsive. A child who has no incentive to move will not move unless he is encouraged to find pleasure in new experiences — even if it is only to shake a rope and jingle bells or have his bare feet plunged into sand or water! For instance, he may be partially sighted and should be encouraged to gain enough confidence to climb on apparatus and learn to use his body so that 'feeling' movement becomes a compensation for seeing that he is climbing. His basic needs are sensory. This special child needs someone to fondle, touch, tickle him; someone to make sounds, talk and stimulate his hearing; someone who will present him with new tastes and smells purely and simply as an experience. The rest of the school, particularly the child in one of the older classes, can help the Special Care child. He should be encouraged to make a picture or mobile to brighten the Special Care classroom; go and visit him occasionally with a shell or pine-cone from the nature table, or a colourful picture from a magazine. He could also make a rattle for him during a suitable music session, the whole aim being to involve the Special Care child in the school's activities; to make him feel an integral part of the school and not, as so often happens, a separate unit in the same building.

In the following chapters the child's needs are discussed more comprehensively and many suggestions are made regarding the different subjects taught in ESNs schools. It is hoped that the reader will be able to utilize these within her own classroom and thus be able to extend her timetable. Several ideas will be found useful for individual teaching, while some, obviously, will be more suitable for group activities. The ideas produced should not, however, be read as a rigid scheme of work to follow, but only as a general guide, leading perhaps to different and further ideas which may come from within the classroom.

Towards the end of the book a list of themes has been compiled for use either within the confines of the classroom or throughout the school. Many points for discussion are listed, including suggestions for follow-up ideas and visits, most of which have been tested and several repeatedly used with different age groups.

It is hoped that some of the suggestions will inspire the young teacher or student and refresh the memory of the well-practised teacher so that they may experiment with ideas of their own and adapt lessons to incorporate their classes' particular needs. If the school as a whole can amalgamate the recent theories and enthusiasm of the young with the knowledge and skill of the older, more experienced teachers, then a school should evolve whereby enough fresh material is available to provide a continually interesting and versatile environment for every child. In this way the child will derive maximum benefit from his teachers and will learn to lead an easier and more enlightened life.

2 The child's needs

One of the fundamental differences between the normal child and the mentally handicapped child is the latter's disinclination to learn. The normal child has an inbuilt instinct to play, explore, discover and learn, which the handicapped child only has to a lesser degree. He will certainly play, explore and discover many new activities, but he is sometimes unable to remember these experiences and hence unable to benefit from them without constant stimulation and reminders from his teacher. What happened yesterday? What did you do? Where did you go? During this situation the teacher should encourage each child to answer in sentences, not monosyllables, which sometimes come more easily to the mentally handicapped child. He tends to think it is sufficient to use one word or gestures in order to be understood and this is often all that's expected of him. The teacher should encourage communication and expect a wider response to her questions. Everything the child has done or is going to do needs to be reinforced and his wider use of language emphasized, as well as encouragement given to him to remember and learn from his own experiences. It is vital that the teacher uses all methods at her disposal to extract as much information as possible from each child.

Sometimes it seems that the child has great difficulty in recalling past events and it is simply 'too much trouble' for him to think. However, if stimulated and encouraged enough he will learn, and will remember. Often in an ESNs school a child has a particular whim and will remember certain facts – like the boy who remembers most of the footballers' names and their relevant teams, or the one who knows many famous TV personalities and the characters they play, or the girl who reads the labels on records that famous pop stars make. Each child remembers what he wants to remember because he is interested in that particular topic. It is up to the teacher to stimulate interest in other things and help him remember them also.

Hence a discussion period each day is valuable to every class.

Routine topics should be discussed, like the day, date, weather, number of children, girls or boys, and the timetable for that day. Any news should also be included; for instance, TV programmes, food, Jane's new dress, or Brian's new shoes. The child can also be encouraged to look forward to a visit or music lesson or talk about a previous painting or cookery session. Daily assembly provides an excellent opportunity for the headteacher to talk to the children about current events, such as a Royal Wedding or the Olympics, as well as annual events such as Easter, Christmas and Harvest time. Once again it is up to each teacher to reinforce the headteacher's points and discuss these in class.

It is also important to the ESNs child that he has time to get to know his teacher, to understand what she expects from him and how to respond to those expectations. At the same time the teacher must beware of becoming too emotionally involved with him. This is sometimes difficult to avoid as the mentally handicapped child is naturally affectionate; but he has enough emotional involvement with his family and needs a more detached involvement from his teacher. It is very easy for her to become jealous of relationships the child may make with other adults and not so easy to be objective. Hence a balance has to be maintained and this can be helped a good deal if teachers are encouraged to change classes fairly frequently – every two or three years perhaps. This would benefit not only the child, who would acquire new interests through a teacher with a different approach, but also the teacher, who would become more experienced at handling different age groups throughout the school and have a more skilful approach to assessing each child's needs. Another way to help the teacher become objective about assessing each child's needs and achievements is to devise fairly simple tests which will show the attainment of the child, as well as provide a guide to the success or otherwise of teaching methods. Various suggestions for tests and ways of carrying them out are discussed towards the end of this book.

It may seem superfluous to remark that the timetable plays an essential part in the daily routine of a well-organized ESNs school. However, without a well-defined routine, each child – especially the young one – will become confused. He has to learn order and discipline. He needs to know that when he has taken off his coat he first goes to the toilet, then he can sit down and drink his milk. This is the routine. Everything has a sequence and eventually he will learn the routine and it will become a habit. Likewise, the older child should learn the weekly routine: for example, on Tuesday he goes swimming, Thursday is cookery day, whilst on Mondays he uses the apparatus in the gym. Thus a weekly routine should evolve throughout the school.

Whilst it may seem contradictory to vary this timetable in any way, it can be refreshing to both the teacher and the child if some of the routine within the classroom is occasionally revised. It should be taken into consideration, however, that the changes involve only a particular class and will not adversely affect the rest of the school. Thus each teacher can employ an alternative timetable at regular intervals, say every six months, or even once a term to suit both her needs and those of her class.

Table 1 (pages 14–17) has been formulated purely as a guide to help teachers assess the approximate intellectual needs of each age group in the school. These observations should be regarded as milestones to aim for, but the groups and ages should not be taken too literally as it often happens that the older child may not have reached a goal that the younger child has attained.

As has been observed, the needs of a mentally handicapped child are as varied as the needs of a normal child, but he also needs additional support, understanding, sympathy and a tolerable amount of patience from his teacher.

Table I

Areas of development	Intellect	Language	Number
Reception	Recognizes familiar people and objects.	Aware of noise. Responds to name.	May understand big and little.
C.A. $3^1/_2$–6 yrs M.A. 12 mths–2 yrs	Watches activities of others with interest.	Babbles a good deal. Understands simple commands.	Plays with nesting boxes, etc. Begins to understand variation in size.
	May be curious.	May learn teacher's name.	
Infants	Able to make needs known. Enjoys simple picture book. Tells boy from girl. Learns new routine quickly.	Jargon, repetition, echolalia. May know other children's names and may name familiar objects, and wrongly name colours.	Begins to sort and match objects. Rote counting. Will grade sizes with more accuracy. One-to-one correspondence.
C.A. 7–9 yrs M.A. 2–3 yrs			

Play	Manipulation	Mobility	Self-help
Solitary. Explores water and sand. Knocks over towers. May imitate adult's action of shaking toy. Plays peek-a-boo.	Explores large toys – no fine coordination. May scribble – grasps crayon awkwardly.	Runs unsteadily. Begins to climb. Pushes and pulls large toys. Sits on trike – pushing feet along floor. Stairs – two feet together.	May become toilet trained. Pulls down own pants. May pull pants up, coat off, shoes off, socks off. Feeds self with spoon.
Parallel play. May play in small groups. Uses cars, bricks, dolls, shop, Wendy House. Imaginative and constructive.	Can pick up small objects. May put right shape into holes with effort. May thread large bricks/beads. Scribbles circular shapes. Holds scissors incorrectly and tries to cut.	Runs steadily. Climbs well. Up steps – alternate feet; down – two feet together. Jumps both feet together. Rides trike with both feet pushing pedals.	Puts on coat. Puts on shoes. Takes off jumper. Unfastens buttons, zips, etc. Plugs in sink, turns taps on, washes hands. Uses knife and fork.

Table 1 (contd)

Areas of development	Intellect	Language	Number
Juniors C.A. 10–13 yrs M.A. 3–4 yrs	May understand some prepositions – up, down, in, out, etc. Understands meaning of tomorrow. Recognizes own written name. Knows age.	Phrases and even sentences. May name primary colours. Will recite days of week. May know today's date.	Counts 1–5 + . Sorts colours and shapes. Understands more than, less than.
Seniors C.A. 13–16 yrs M.A. 4–5 + yrs	Understands passage of time e.g. last week, next week. May know birthday. Recognizes few words (written). Should know home address.	Names most colours. Sorts all colours. May know date. Recites months of year.	May recognize number symbol and add single numbers. Knows value of coins, e.g. 10p, 5p, 2p. Understands most words describing relative size and quantity – narrow, wide, high, low, etc.

Postage will be paid by licensee
Do not affix Postage Stamps if posted in Great Britain, Channel Islands, or Northern Ireland

Ward Lock Educational Co. Ltd.
116 Baker Street
London W1E 2EZ

Teaching Mentally Handicapped Children

OTHER TITLES WHICH MAY INTEREST YOU

You may examine any of the books listed below for 30 days without being under any obligation. Simply tick the titles of your choice, stating which volume required where applicable, fill in your name and address, and drop this card in the post.

Publication SEPTEMBER 1978

Art and Craft for Primary Schools
Annette Wood

☐ **£3.75** hb approx.

Publication SEPTEMBER 1978

The Funny Family and Other Songs, Games and Rhymes for Children
Alison McMorland

☐ **£3.50** hb approx.

Helping Children with Learning Difficulties
A Diagnostic Teaching Approach
Denis H. Stott

☐ **£6.50** hb   ☐ **£3.25** pb

Pictures and Conversations
Resources for Language Development
Books 1-3
Nora Wilkinson

Remedial Education
Objectives and Techniques
John McCreesh and Austen Maher

☐ **£2.75** hb   ☐ **£1.35** pb

Schools Council Communications Skills in Early Childhood Project
Listening to Children Talking
A Guide to the Appraisal of Children's Use of Language
Joan Tough

☐ **£3.00** hb   ☐ **£1.95** pb

Talking and Learning
A Guide to Fostering Communication Skills
Joan Tough

☐ **£6.00** hb   ☐ **£2.95** pb

Underprivileged Underfives
Lorna Bell

☐ **£2.25** pb

☐ **Please send me your current catalogue**
☐ **Please arrange for a representative to call**

INSPECTION COPIES ONLY SENT WITHIN UK

NAME . . . .

ADDRESS . . . .

. . . .

Play	Manipulation	Mobility	Self-help
Very sociable, dramatic and imaginative. Associates with 'pop' stars and TV characters. May learn to play hide and seek.	Is fairly competent at familiar table games. Can pour well. Copies shapes and even name. Draws/paints dots, circles, strokes and often recognizable pictures. Can cut.	Hops, skips, stands on one leg. Very skilful at climbing and riding trike. Walks on tiptoe. Dances to music.	Fastens buttons, press-studs. Washes hands/ face. Cares about appearance – combs hair. Uses knife/fork correctly. Washes and dries pots. Spreads butter on bread.
Still sociable. May have 'special' boy or girl friend. May become self-conscious. Often 'fashion' conscious (girls) and needs to follow current trend in sport, 'pop' or TV. Can learn team games.	Can write name. Pictures more imaginative. Can cut out pictures. May thread needle, hand/eye coordination very skilful.	May lose some confidence when climbing. May learn to ride two-wheeled bike.	Fastens zips, press-studs, sometimes shoe laces. Sets table. Clears and wipes table. Brews tea, makes toast. *Girls* wash smalls, change own napkin. *Boys* clean shoes.

Part 2

Creative Activities

3 Art

As previously observed, it is vital that every experience the child has is reinforced and emphasized in the classroom. Here creativity plays an important role, and from the child's point of view art is often one of the most enjoyable activities he pursues. It gives the teacher an ideal opportunity to follow up other school activities and very often the child will be able to take his work home so that his parents too will be able to talk to him about his various experiences. However, it can be one of the most laborious lessons to organize. So much preparation is involved, particularly if there is no assistant in the classroom. Modern liquid paints and PVA glue have lessened much of this preparation, as they are often kept in ready-to-use containers and need no mixing.

The teacher can also save herself time if she can keep a good supply of assorted collage materials within easy reach. Empty plastic sweet jars are very serviceable and could, for example, hold lentils, pasta, bottle-tops, ready-cut scraps of cloth and paper shapes – all clearly seen, easy to get out and ready for use. An additional and valuable exercise would be to give a child the task of refilling the containers when necessary.

Many teachers plan their classrooms so that the child can select his own activity at least for part of the day, in which case it will be most convenient if all the materials and tools are kept together. Then when a child wishes to cut out or crayon he can go to a certain shelf or cupboard and find assorted sizes of ready-cut paper, scissors, glue, crayons, paint and brushes all ready for use. Nearly every child can be taught how to wash out his brushes and return all his tools to the correct place after use.

Sometimes it may be beneficial for the teacher to have a more directed situation whereby she shows the class, or a group within the class, how to paint a simple face, for example. From this directed instruction the child can learn basic shapes, patterns and number. It can be reinforced by each child creating a face of his own, either by copying the teacher's picture, using a mirror, or looking at other faces in the classroom and choosing his own materials to work with. The child is not only developing self-expression but he is also learning manipulation, the art of controlling his paint brush and a certain amount of visual perception, all of which skills will help him move towards leading a more independent life as he grows older. The child should be allowed to create a spontaneous picture of his own determination at another time so that there is room in every environment for both formal and informal creativity, and the experienced teacher will be able to adjust to either, as the situation demands.

However, it should be noted that if the ambitious teacher is going in for a large full-scale project then a mentally handicapped child will not often have the patience to participate. He becomes bored with anything that is not finished fairly quickly. The making up of a model village, for example, may involve the use of large amounts of papier mâché, for which even the older child cannot retain enough interest to complete the project. Sometimes it takes days, or even weeks, for layer upon layer of newspaper and glue to dry out, and papier mâché made in a hurry isn't at all successful. There are many suitable substitutes around these days and it is up to the teacher to seek out and use the quicker alternatives.

Simplicity and speed are both essential elements of all creative activities with the mentally handicapped, especially as the teacher's aim is to maintain the child's interest while expanding his language, skills, knowledge and understanding. The work he does, therefore, should be completed as carefully and promptly as possible in order that his teacher can display it most effectively at the earliest opportunity.

The following pages contain ideas for creative activities – for both group and individual sessions – dealing with painting, cutting, drawing, collage, and the chapter ends with a few hints on displaying all art work to the best advantage.

Painting

Basic painting, using only a brush, some paper and paint is a very simple activity from which all children derive a great deal of pleasure.

The mentally handicapped child is no exception. He enjoys painting from an early age and it can be most rewarding to observe the maturing of his pictures as he moves through the school. His first attempts at painting will merely involve a few hesitant dabs on the paper; later he will learn how to make more interesting strokes and use many different colours to achieve attractive patterns. Often an ESNs child may develop a particular flair for painting and will produce excellent pictures well above the general standard for his approximate mental age.

Painting is not a difficult lesson to organize, though it is often more successful if only a small group is painting at once, particularly when dealing with the younger child. It has also been found through experience that the younger child enjoys painting on a flat surface such as a table, rather than an upright easel which an older child often prefers. Whichever age group is being considered it is essential that every child wears some form of protective clothing and that a damp cloth is always kept close at hand.

Modern paint

The modern liquid paint in a squeeze bottle is most useful, comes in many bright colours which fade very little, and doesn't usually dry out in the paint jar. It can be used straight from the bottle, thickened with paste, watered down, or, if mixed with PVA glue and then watered down, has an excellent adhesive quality which covers shiny boxes, margarine pots and yoghurt cartons effectively in one coat. Unfortunately it has been found that the orange, purple and black in these paints will not wash out of clothing once it has dried, so it is once again essential to keep a damp cloth within easy reach.

Powder paint

This type of paint is now regarded by many as old fashioned, but it shouldn't be completely ignored, as it still has many uses along with the more modern paints. It is particularly useful for mixing with grainy substances such as sand or powder paste which, when combined and mixed with water, produce a very effective, textured picture. It can also be used as a powder and sprinkled carefully onto a moist surface which makes quite an attractive speckled background for a bolder design.

All kinds of painted pictures can be enhanced as well as protected from fading if covered with a watered-down PVA glue when dry, thus giving the whole picture a varnished appearance.

Different utensils to use with paint

thick brushes	foam sponges
thin brushes	loofahs
toothbrushes	rollers
nailbrushes	straws – thick and thin
combs – large and small	string
doyleys	stencils

Different effects with paint

Background wash (7–16 years)

Water is soaked over the paper with a clean brush. The child quickly covers the paper with paint, which runs into the water, producing a pleasing effect, particularly when various colours are used. If blue is chosen this can be used as a background to make a very effective pale sky. Blue powder paint could be sprinkled over the watery surface to produce an alternative background.

Blow painting (10–16 years)

With a straw the child blows the paint across his paper. This is a very difficult skill for the ESNs child, though it is an excellent exercise for him to practise as he needs to learn to blow and breathe properly. The best results have been achieved with *Art Straws* (cut in half) as these are thicker than most drinking straws. For a similar effect, which is easier to achieve, see *Drizzle painting*.

Butterfly painting (all ages)

This is a very simple technique any child in any class should be able to do. The child daubs thick paint over one half of a sheet of paper, and the paper is then folded in half (preferably by the teacher if she is dealing with a younger child). When the paper is opened out again the symmetrical design which is revealed is most attractive, particularly if several different colours of paint have been used. If necessary, the teacher can draw the outline of a butterfly round the painting to emphasize the design.

Comb painting (all ages)

For this to be really successful the paint should be thickened with paste and a fairly heavy paper should be used. The paper is thickly covered with different colours of paint. Each child then draws a large-toothed comb through the paint in waves and swirls. This can be quite effective done on a large scale, as well as with small individual pictures. The 'tail' of a tail-comb can be used too, but this will not be as effective as the multiple parallel tracks, which give a 3-D appearance to the picture.

Drizzle painting

This produces a very attractive effect as well as being one of the easiest techniques to achieve and can be successful either on a large or a small scale.

Large scale (all ages). If it is convenient for every child to sit around a large sheet of paper on the floor, it will be easier than trying to use the table. Different colours of paint should be squirted onto the paper by the teacher and each child in turn can hold up part of the picture, allowing the paint to 'drizzle' across the paper. This is an easy large-scale picture that every child – even the partially sighted and Special Care child – seems to enjoy.

Small scale (10–16 years). With the older child it may be more appropriate for him to make a small individual drizzle picture on the table top, providing he learns not to squeeze too much paint out and is able to tip the paper in all directions without drizzling all over the table.

Finger painting (all ages)

Only a very highly organized teacher would attempt this with a large group, whereby every child has his fingers covered with paint at the same time. Finger painting does, however, provide a wonderful opportunity for the child to explore the texture and substance of this liquid medium. It is good for him to understand that he is allowed to play with the paint – at a certain time. Sometimes, however, there may be a child who does not like having messy hands and wants to wash his fingers as soon as they are dirty. It is equally important for him to be encouraged to play with the paint as it is for the rest of the group.

Bearing these points in mind it is often easier if finger painting is kept to an individual session – particularly with the more adventurous younger child – so that the teacher, or her assistant, is in full control of the situation. It is also strongly recommended that the child wears a fairly substantial form of protective clothing.

Many attractive patterns can be developed from hand prints. For example, large flowers can be made using red or yellow hand prints for petals, green hand prints for leaves and maybe brown ones for the plant roots. The older child could cut out his 'hand' print and the group could paste together several hands, all shapes and sizes, forming a regular pattern. For example, they could be pasted into a circle and made to look like the sun, or green ones could be glued to form a triangle to represent a Christmas tree. A giant's hand could be cut out of strong paper and covered with hand prints and cut-outs in contrasting colours. The possibilities of designs using the hand as a basic pattern are almost endless.

Finger printing. A simple but effective print can be taken from a finger painting if a flat hard base is available. The base can be any shape, but a circle is particularly effective. The child makes a pattern in the paint on the base, then a piece of paper is smoothed over the paint by the teacher, thus producing a reprint. The child can carry on playing in the paint whilst his picture is drying.

There are many other possibilities with finger painting but it is worth noting that black paint is to be avoided at all costs because it becomes so ingrained in the grooves of mongols' hands that it takes hours of soaking to get them clean. If black and white contrasts are required then white paint should be used on black paper. The same advice is obviously recommended for foot painting too.

Spatter painting (10–16 years)

This is another interesting technique for use as a background for pictures – particularly on cards, for example at Easter or Christmas. An old toothbrush or small nailbrush is dipped in some paint, a ruler is then drawn carefully across the bristles, thus spattering the paint over the paper. Sometimes it is easier if the child uses his finger instead of the ruler, as he has more control. To prevent too much waste and paint being spattered far and wide, it is quite useful to place the paper into a box and spatter the paint over the paper, so that the excess paint is trapped in the box. This is particularly effective if templates are initially attached to the paper. For example, an Easter chicken, a star or an angel for Christmas, can be cut out of card and held on to the paper while paint is spattered around it. When the template is removed, a silhouette is revealed – where, if desired, the greetings can be written.

String painting (7–16 years)

The following method of string painting is more effective than twirling pieces of painted string over a piece of paper, which is hard to control and doesn't produce an interesting picture, even when done by the senior class.

Cut different lengths of string for each colour to be used. Dip the string in the paint and place it carefully in a wavy line over one side of the paper. The teacher should then fold the paper in half over the string, placing a firm hand on the top. The child then pulls the string. These produce very effective 'streaky' pictures for individual work, but need a good deal of organization for a larger group project.

Wax painting (all ages)
The most popular type of wax painting is called 'wax-resist', when each child presses a wax crayon deeply into a piece of stiff paper and then paints over the crayoning with watery paint. An attractive design can be made if the child crayons over a raised surface like heavy wallpaper for example. The subsequent painting will then imitate the wallpaper design. Every child will not be able to press down hard enough with his crayons and it may be necessary, particularly in the case of the younger child, for the teacher to help him press down − but nearly every child should be able to paint over his picture and each will be delighted to see the wax resist the paint.

The very talented child may even be able to draw a picture − a face or a house − using a candle so that the crayoning won't show, and paint over the paper in order to reveal the picture.

Printing (all ages)
The designs and patterns made by paint, using anything but a brush, are usually referred to as printing. It is a most satisfactory artistic medium, especially with the ESNs child who really only has to be able to press − or even pat − down gently to create an interesting pattern with contrasting shapes and designs. The best and most suitable containers for the paint when printing are chip-shop trays. These are usually made out of polystyrene and will wash, store neatly and are big enough to hold all but the biggest printing mediums. All they need is a piece of sponge in the base to absorb the paint and the excess moisture. Any flat shape of wood can be used for a base if the teacher is to make her own printing blocks, and the string, lino or foam pieces should be glued or nailed firmly in place so that the print will make an attractive pattern.

The handles for these printing blocks can vary enormously according to the child's needs in each class. For example, a simple cotton-reel is often used − though these are not always sufficient for clumsy or spastic fingers. The large cone-shaped bobbins are often easier to use and they can be successfully attached to the block with strong PVA glue or *Polyfilla*. Another fairly simple handle to make is a large, broad piece of elastic nailed to both sides of a block of wood.

This is especially useful in the Special Care classes as the child does not need to concentrate on holding the printing block, and can still make a reasonable picture.

Some items which have been found to be very useful for creating attractive designs in printing are listed below.

Different utensils to use for printing

Natural
    fruit: apples, pears, lemons, oranges – cut in half
    vegetables: carrots, potatoes – shapes cut out of them; leeks, onions
        – cut in half
    leaves
    hands
    feet

Teacher- or man-made
    rulers
    matchboxes (open end)   } an attractive combination of
    empty toilet-roll tubes   shapes, long and short lines,
    empty *Sellotape* rolls } and circles

    rolled-up newspaper   wooden cotton-reels
    string, wound around a tin   yoghurt pots
    swirls and shapes of string   *Dinky* cars rolled over painted
        stuck onto flat, firm surface   surface
    foam rubber shapes stuck onto   almost anything rolled over
        same   painted surface
    PVA lumps of glue stuck onto   plant pots – *not* plastic
        same   sponges
    lino shapes stuck onto same   soles of shoes/plimsoles

Collage

Collage is the word used to describe any kind of picture or design made from assorted materials. The picture can be a scene like the seaside, a lone figure (for example a clown or animal), or even a chart for everyday use, like the weather chart. Colour and simplicity should be the main themes for all collages. An attractive eye-catching picture made out of anything from lentils to scraps of cloth or from cellophane to sequins can make even the dullest classroom bright and cheerful to work in.

When initially composing the picture it is important to think of several factors. First, the colour and shape of the medium to be used should complement the colour and shape of the picture – for example, butter beans and newspaper would be unsuitable for the bright colours necessary to create a clown. Second, remember where the picture is to be displayed, and consider the weight of the finished collage. For example, Cinderella's coach was once made out of pasta, peas, lentils and sequins – and a huge, magnificent coach it was – but unfortunately it was unable to be displayed to advantage as the drawing pins were useless on plaster walls and the picture was far too heavy to be supported by *Sellotape* or *Blu-Tack*. Eventually it rested on top of a cupboard in a rather dark corner and was hardly seen.

As previously mentioned, collage work can be either formal or informal. Less preparation is required for the latter, just backing paper, glue, assorted materials placed on a suitable table in the classroom, and each child can be allowed to create his own designs. If the teacher is following a certain theme, however, it is advisable for her to direct the child's picture, particularly in the case of the younger or less capable child. He loves to make pictures, but is also very impetuous and, if left with a pot of glue, will paste everything in sight – his hair, hands, face, clothes, table – in fact everything except the picture! It will be obvious to all but the least experienced, therefore, that the teacher of this child will need to spread the glue for him onto the picture in the desired place. As he learns through lots of practice, the child will become more discriminating and eventually it will probably only be necessary for the teacher to outline the basic shape in a thick felt-tip pen, leaving the child to create the remainder of the picture himself. Once again, PVA glue has proved invaluable for its instant and efficient adhesive quality, whether it is used neat for pasta or watered down for thin cloth scraps and paper. It can also give a very attractive finish to pasta pictures if the top of the pasta is pasted, giving it a varnished appearance.

Lists of useful collage materials are given below.

Paper

tissue
coloured, sticky
cellophane
coloured cellophane

} particularly useful if cut up into shapes – circles, squares, triangles and kept in ready-to-use container, e.g. old plastic sweet jar

crêpe (colour may run if
     watery paste is used)
newspaper
kitchen towels
N.B. Scrap paper is usually available free from paper
manufacturers.

tin foil
wallpaper
coloured metallic paper

Food
Dried
barley
butter beans
kidney beans
lentils
split peas
black-eyed peas
peas
bird seed

rice, sago, tapioca
cornflakes, etc.
pasta – look for butterfly
     shapes, snails, curly, spirals
spaghetti
lasagne – plain or green
macaroni
noodles

Washed and dried
apple pips   melon seeds
orange pips   orange skin
grape pips   grapefruit skin   pressed flat then cut
date stones   pineapple skin   into interesting shape
plum stones   melon skin
N.B. Any of the pale colours above can be decorated by painting
(add PVA glue to paint) or dyed with a little food colouring added to
boiling water. (Immerse pasta for a few seconds then remove and
leave to dry.)

Cloth scraps
(useful if kept in containers, cut up into small pieces ready to use)
velvet, crushed   cotton
velvet, corduroy   silk
leather   nylon
suede   fibreglass
woollens   fur fabric
tweed   net curtaining
Crimplene   felt

Waste materials
(useful for large model-making, castles, trains, etc.)

cartons
toilet-roll tubes
kitchen-towel tubes
yoghurt pots
margarine pots
cheese-boxes (good for wheels)
washing-up liquid bottles
cotton-reels (good for wheels)
milk-bottle tops
metal bottle tops

shells
straws
broken tiles
lino
spent matches
matchboxes
egg-boxes
plastic milk bottles
plastic long-life milk bottles
    (different shape)
empty *Sellotape* tubes

Dressmaking scraps

buttons
buckles
curtain rings
sequins
beads
knitting wool (yarn)

raffia
lace
cotton-wool
feathers
embroidery silks

Do-it-yourself scraps

sawdust
sandpaper
wood shavings (attractive for
    curly hair)
wire (useful in model-making)
string

sand
screws, nuts, bolts
nails
polystyrene pieces
lino offcuts

Dried plant material

pressed flowers ⎫ colour retained if preserved in Borax
pressed petals ⎰ (3–4 weeks) or silica-gel (3–4 days)

leaves, green, pressed
honesty
grasses, assorted
rose-hips – dried
bark – silver birch attractive
orange peel ⎫
grapefruit peel etc. ⎰ cut to oval shapes and dried flat
beech leaves – turn coppery if preserved in glycerine. (Stand stems
    in 1 part glycerine – 2 parts hot water; takes 2–3 weeks.)

Sources of pictures

(good to copy for collage ideas)

children's crayoning books

greeting cards, wrapping
paper

children's storybooks

Sunday colour supplements

women's magazines

centrefold pictures in teachers'
magazines

children's comics

children's cartoon comics

} good for collection of assorted photos
for different themes

Drawing and cutting

Aids to manipulation

Drawing with crayons or pencils is just as important for the ESNs child as painting. In fact, it is through drawing that he learns the art of manipulation and fine control of his finger muscles. He will never learn to copy shapes or write his own name unless he has first explored all the properties and possibilities of scribbling with a pencil or crayon. He has to learn how to hold the pencil so that it is both comfortable and well controlled, and he can only learn this with a great deal of practice. Drawing helps the child develop a good coordination between his hand and eye – and it is one of the first ways in which the observant teacher will be able to discern if the child needs to wear glasses.

The art of controlling the crayon is a great help to the child when he begins to manipulate small objects like hammering nails, fastening buttons or even threading needles. The frequent use of a crayon or pencil can play a large part in helping the handicapped child acquire good hand–eye coordination which is essential if he is to lead a more independent life.

As with drawing, cutting too is an important skill which will help to improve the child's coordination and manipulation. It is, however, a much more difficult skill to teach. The teacher needs to stand behind the child in order to teach him how to hold the scissors correctly, yet he must not be expected to learn in only one or two sessions. The child will never learn to cut if he is given blunt scissors and thin paper or cloth; it is essential that he has sharp scissors, fairly stiff paper and daily opportunities to practise cutting. Whenever possible a cutting table should be available in the classroom. Experience has shown accidents are rare — except for the boy who once unfortunately practised cutting his own hair!

As previously noted, cutting is a difficult skill to accomplish, particularly when the child wants to cut around a picture. Once he has developed the necessary skills, however, many more creative pictures can be developed and designed, both to enliven the child and to enhance the environment.

Opposite are lists of suitable drawing utensils, their uses and several attractive techniques which involve cutting and a description of how to accomplish them.

Display of hand shapes (page 46)

Butterfly paintings (page 23)

Mosaic pictures (page 37)

Faces (see *Themes*)

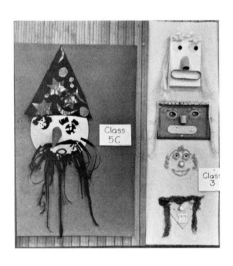

(*left*) Blow painting, a creative activity which helps to teach correct breathing (page 23)

(*below*) Cutting is an important manipulative skill (note the special scissors for hands with poor muscle control) (page 31)

Drawing utensils

Utensil	Advantages	Disadvantages	Techniques
Biro	Usually smudge-proof. Writes fine lines.	Will not erase. Needs pressure.	Copying, writing on top, drawing.
Pencil	Little pressure needed. Will erase.	Dull, colourless lines. Needs frequent sharpening.	Scribbling, rubbing, drawing, writing on top. Compass, template, set square.
Charcoal	No pressure needed.	Very brittle. Smudges badly.	Rubbing, drawing.
Chalk	No pressure needed. Various colours. Will erase.	Smudges. Very dusty.	Child can draw, then erase, draw again. Rubbing, prints.
Felt-tip	Many bright colours. Thick or thin available. (Valve type lasts longest.)	Some not waterproof. Will not erase. Tip may dry out quickly.	Copying, writing on top, colouring, outlines, drawing. Template, set square.
Coloured pencil	Fine lines.	Much pressure needed. Regular sharpening.	Scribbling, writing on top, copying, drawing. Template, set square.
Wax crayon	Many bright colours. Thin and thick.	Will not erase.	Rubbing, rolling, colouring, carved, wax resist, drawing.

Techniques with crayons

Rubbing (7–16 years)

This is a fairly simple technique which produces attractive results with very little preparation. An interesting pattern evolves when a crayon or pencil is rubbed over a roughened or relief surface, such as some wallpapers. A clean sheet of paper should be taped or stapled to the rough surface and the child rubs a crayon very hard over the paper. Rubbing is most successful if thick wax crayons are used and attractive pictures can come simply by rubbing over wallpaper designs. However, the younger child may find this very difficult as the crayon requires a great deal of pressure. It may be easier for him to rub over a solitary raised shape rather than a series of patterns. For instance, a template of an animal could be used. It could be wooden or cut out of lino and should be placed under a piece of paper and well secured. The child rubs over the paper with pencil, charcoal or chalk and produces a very effective animal in silhouetted form.

A different rubbing activity suitable for the older child involves rubbing with charcoal or a pencil onto fairly thin paper over 2p, 5p, 10p and 50p coins – thus extending his knowledge and improving his coin recognition.

It is also interesting for each child to take a bark, fence or stone rubbing when out in the countryside. Fairly thick paper and charcoal are best for this activity although the teacher should not expect the examples to be of a high standard. On return to school they can be displayed on or near the nature table and appropriately labelled. It is unlikely that the child will comprehend the difference between the trees, but he should be able to discern which rubbing was taken from a rough surface and which was taken from a smooth one. Additionally the teacher should try to provide some pieces of bark or stones (she could bring some back from the countryside visit) in order that the same activity may be carried on in the classroom – indeed, the results should be more interesting, as the child will have more time and comfort in which to produce his rubbings.

Taking a line for a walk or *Scribbling* (all ages)

This describes very accurately a simple activity whereby the child draws a single line and, never taking the pencil off the paper, creates curves and swirls in a variety of shapes and sizes. He can then chalk or crayon inside the shapes in assorted colours thus producing a very pleasing abstract design. The older child may see a design in his scribble – like a face or an animal.

Carved crayon (7–16 years)
A thick wax crayon is used for this technique, and large pieces are carved out of the side of it by the teacher. The child then rolls and rubs the carved crayon across the paper and parallel stripes of colour are produced which the child learns to sweep and swirl to look more effective. Once again, however, a certain amount of pressure is needed and the older child will find it easier than the younger child.

Chalk prints (7–16 years)
Initially chalk should be rubbed over a piece of paper. Then place a piece of black paper over the chalked surface. Very carefully fold the two papers in half, then quarters. (It is probably best if the teacher does this, otherwise the chalk may smudge and spoil the picture.) Smooth the papers together with the palm of a hand. Mark lines and curves on the folded paper, pressing down hard with a hard edged utensil, like a ruler. Carefully open out the paper and the chalk should be reprinted onto the black paper, with lines scored through it creating the same pattern in each quarter. A more effective picture can be created if different colours of chalk are used.

Copying (7–16 years)
It is through copying that the child learns to recognize and discriminate between shapes and the beginnings of understanding reading and writing may be evolved. Whilst it is obvious that few ESNs children ever learn to read fluently, they often need to recognize different shapes and numbers. For example, they will need to learn name recognition, local bus numbers and later food packages in supermarkets. Here are some basic shapes which the child may learn to copy:

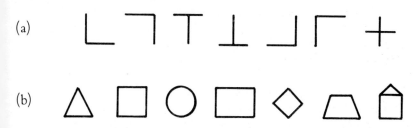

The (a) set of shapes could be copied with spent matches or *Art Straws* if the child has difficulty in holding crayons. Each teacher will be able to introduce more complex shapes as the child develops.

Writing on top (10–16 years)
This is another way in which the child can learn to control his crayon
as a prelude to reading and writing. The teacher dots out a shape or
word for the child to 'write on top'.

(a) My name is John

(b) My name is John

It is not really necessary to discuss any further methods of pre-
reading/writing techniques as many books have been written on this
subject, and if the teacher feels the child is ready for more complex
exercises more information will be found elsewhere. It is sufficient to
observe that the child is often capable of learning many more
academic activities than he is given credit for.

Templates, rulers, set squares, etc. (13–16 years)
If a child has learnt to reproduce a shape by drawing around a
template, there is no reason why he could not learn to use a ruler, set
square, or even a protractor in the same manner. Many delightful
patterns can be made by using these instruments, which would be too
symmetrical for the child to create free-hand. A compass, too, is very
rarely seen in ESNs schools, yet with practice a child could learn how
to use it. Perhaps he could even learn to make large and small circles;
it will all improve his manipulation and indeed may help him to
appreciate patterns with a symmetrical design. The teacher could help
the younger child by duplicating coloured, interesting shapes to help
the child create ideas of his own. No child can develop fully if he is left
to discover designs and patterns by himself – he does need to be
shown, and even if he is incapable of reproducing symmetry he can be
encouraged to appreciate it.

Techniques with scissors

Jigsaw pictures (7–16 years)
Once the child has learnt to cut along a straight line he can make
jigsaw pictures. Wide parallel lines should be marked on the back of a
picture. The child then cuts along these lines until his painting is in

broad strips. With the help of the teacher the child glues the strips, evenly spaced, onto a plain backing sheet, thus producing the simplest form of jigsaw picture. With practice more elaborate designs can be created. For instance, the strips could be set out 'fan-like', close together at the bottom and widely spaced at the top, or the spread could be staggered, closely linked at one side and spread wider apart across the picture. The more skilful child could even cut wavy or curved lines and paste the shapes alternately up and down across a plain sheet of backing paper, thus producing an interesting and dramatic effect.

Mosaic pictures (10–16 years)
Mosaics simply involve filling in an outline with many small pieces of colour. The pieces can be of fabric, paper or any other material, multicoloured or plain, depending on the subject. The small pieces can be cut to any shape, but if it is possible then an even more effective mosaic will be created if every piece is the same shape. This is obviously easier to accomplish with the older child who will be able to cut along lines the teacher has drawn. Mosaics can also be used when teaching number and shape – 'How many small triangles fit into this large one?' for example.

Paper doyleys (7–16 years)
This is a well-used exercise which all children have made since time immemorial! Each child is given a square piece of paper which either he or his teacher folds in four or eight equal parts. The child then cuts corners off and cuts triangular shapes out of the sides of the folded paper. When the paper is opened out many shapes and holes are revealed, thus producing an attractive doyley. This can then be painted for decoration or used as a stencil over another piece of paper.

More paper sculpture (7–16 years)
There are a great many other attractive ways to cut shapes and patterns out of different kinds of paper, some of which are illustrated on page 39.

Paper flowers (all ages)
Paper flowers can add a good deal to almost any picture at any time of the year. In Spring, Summer and at Christmas time flowers can make an ordinary picture much more interesting and colourful, and they are also very popular with mothers when taken home as gifts. The following are just a few very simple ways to make paper flowers:

Windmill

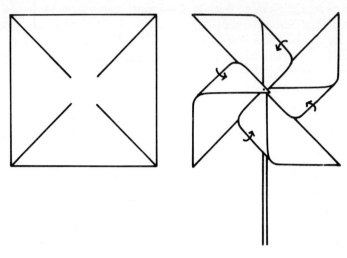

Crown

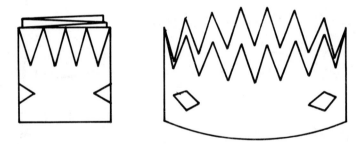

1 Cut out circles of crêpe paper (the teacher can do this for the younger child). Stretch each circle to make it wavy and wind it onto a length of florists' wire. Alternatively it could be glued or pinned directly onto the display board. A bunch of these look very effective in a vase on the teacher's desk.

2 Group tiny Christmas balls together with florists' wire and wind crêpe paper around the balls or push circles of tissue paper up the wire making the balls the flower centre.

3 Cut strips of crêpe paper 2" wide from the bought length. Make several cuts of $1^1/_2$" along the width to provide fringe petals. Begin to wind up the crêpe paper to a flower shape on florists' wire — secure with glue or sticky tape.

(a) Fold paper concertina fashion.

(b) Cut out shape.

(c) Final string of diamonds etc.

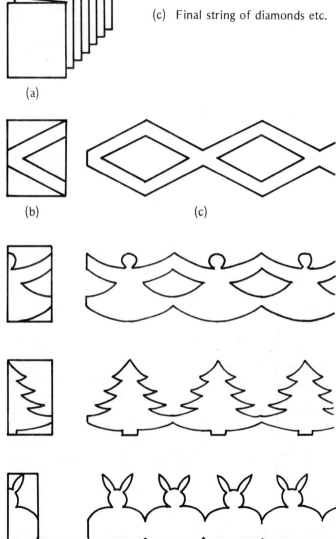

(a)

(b)   (c)

4   Fold a square of gummed paper or tissue paper into eight or sixteen triangles. Make two wavy lines, or several jagged lines near the top of the triangle to produce petals – see Figures 1 and 2. Open out to produce a flower. Varying sizes and assorted colours will produce some very attractive flowers which can either be displayed on a wall or threaded with florists' wire and displayed in a vase. A similar effect can be achieved using circles of tissue paper (see Figure 3).

Symmetrical jigsaw pictures (13–16 years)
Like the jigsaw pictures previously described, these symmetrical ones require a picture or colourful paper for cutting out. A square or oblong picture is most suitable and the teacher will probably have to draw the lines for the child to cut along. These lines can form different shapes, like a square, circle or triangle, or they can all form the same shape.

Figure 1

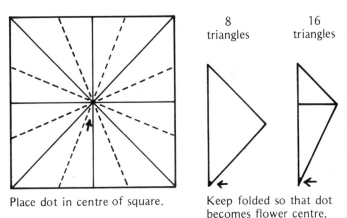

8
triangles

16
triangles

Place dot in centre of square.

Keep folded so that dot becomes flower centre.

Figure 2 (a)

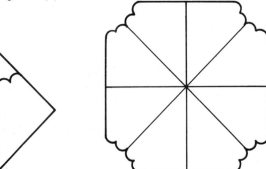

Figure 2 (b)

 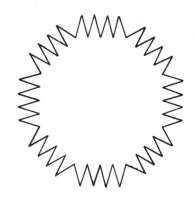

Figure 3

The child should carefully cut along the lines, removing the shape and keeping it on one side. Each piece should be placed on a backing sheet evenly spaced out to its required position (see Figures 4, 5, 6).

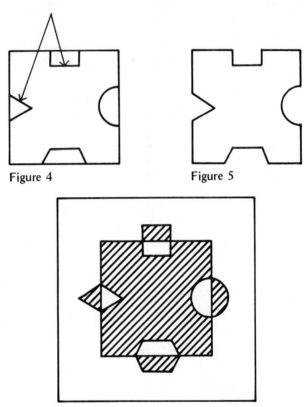

Figure 4   **Figure 5**

Figure 6 Final display showing
symmetry

If a square picture is used then each of the sides could be used for a different shape, a semi-circle, triangle, square and diamond, for instance. This is an excellent activity whereby the child can learn to fit the shapes correctly, in a more sophisticated manner than formboards, which he may have used in younger classes.

The shape can be adjusted according to the teacher's requirements but it can be re-emphasized by cutting squares out of squares, triangles out of triangles, for example (see Figures 7, 8). These are

Figure 7

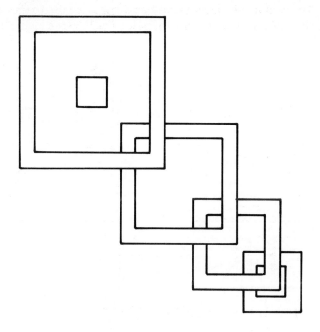

Figure 8

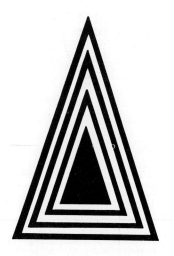

most attractive, but if the lines are very narrow or the paper rather thin it may be more successful for the teacher actually to glue down all but the solid shape.

Mobiles (all ages)

Mobiles are very effective and hold the interest of all ages, particularly the Special Care child, who may be immobile. It is a good idea for the older child to make the mobiles and take them to the child in Special Care, who will probably enjoy the bright colours and watch them moving about. For the same child a tinkling mobile is also very attractive — but is sometimes rather difficult to make. The simplest form of mobile can be a snake spiral. It only requires a spiral cut out of a large circular picture. The centre of the spiral should be threaded onto cotton and suspended from the ceiling.

Figure 9

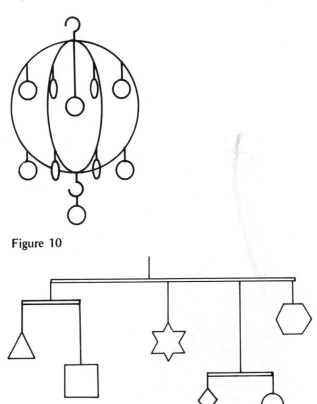

Figure 10

A wire coat-hanger is an excellent medium for displaying more elaborate mobiles. It can be pulled into the shape of a ring. A second coat-hanger can be pushed through the middle, forming a cross-shape. If more hanging space is needed, two could be suspended under the first one and four more beneath these. Ordinary cotton thread is adequate for most mobiles, but nylon thread, wire or plastic is equally suitable. *Art Straws* or plastic drinking straws can be used instead of the hangers, but it is more difficult to establish a correct balance with them (see Figures 9, 10).

Suitable subjects for mobiles

Hallowe'en	*Christmas*	*Easter*
(black silhouettes)	fir trees	bunnies
moon, crescent	stars	chickens
stars	angels	lambs
witch	trumpets	eggs
black cat	three kings	bonnet
broomstick	one giant star	
cauldron	Christmas bells	
pointed hat	foil shapes	

Space	*Shapes*	*Face*
robot	flat or 3-D	hat
spaceship	squares	eyes
moon	triangles	nose
stars	diamonds	moustache
flying saucer	circles	mouth
planets	ovals	bow tie

Miscellaneous	
fish	body parts
birds	buildings
bottles	faces
fruit	flying
musical instruments	insects
hats	sport
Chinese lanterns	transport
animals	

Display

When the art work in school has been completed, even the most impressive projects can be spoiled if they are badly displayed. Likewise, a motley collection of paintings can be greatly improved if grouped together and given an attractive backing. An overall neat and tidy appearance is important. Care should be taken to cut lines straight, when required, and not to hide faulty cutting under folds of paper and dozens of drawing pins.

Labelling is also important for the display to look well finished and care should be taken to write neat, clear labels. If the pictures are to be displayed outside the classroom, then it is important to include the name or number of the class on the label – for example, 'Class 5: Blow Painting', or, within the classroom, 'Autumn Fruits: Group Work'. These labels are not necessarily for the children to read but rather to improve a good display and to provide the visitor with relevant information.

Choosing suitable contrasting colours is another essential method of good displays. Light on dark, or vice-versa, is usually a good rule. For instance, white paintings look attractive on a black or blue background, as do yellow ones, but green or red are not very suitable on a purple backing sheet – there is not enough contrast. It is also interesting to contrast shapes. Curvy pictures enjoy a square background, for instance, and this is a great help to all teachers who have difficulty in cutting straight lines.

A plain backing-sheet of paper covering a wall or a display board is often a quick method of framing many pictures at once. However, there are many more interesting ways to display art work. One way to link butterfly pictures together, for example, is to cut the backing paper to the shape of a giant butterfly and display the paintings, carefully positioned inside. This is a striking design and will immediately catch the eye. In a similar manner hand prints and foot prints could be displayed on a backing sheet cut like a giant's hand or foot, as appropriate. There are many other possibilities for displays following a similar idea.

A special picture could be framed individually, using several frames of various contrasting colours cut into different shapes (see Figures 11, 12).

The theme of a frieze can be emphasized by surrounding the picture with a series of small motifs. For example, an Easter frieze could be bordered with broken eggshells, bunnies or chickens; a Hallowe'en

Figure 11 Informal display of individual picture

an abstract
design
by
Bill

Figure 12 Formal display of individual picture

my house by
Mary

frieze could be bordered with black cats or witches' cauldrons, and there are many other themes which can be emphasized in a similar manner. It can be interesting to provide a 3-D effect for a frieze. Several different-sized cartons and boxes should be covered with wallpaper or scrap paper. These boxes should be hidden from sight but, if successfully displayed, can make certain pictures stand away from the wall, giving a 3-D effect. The boxes can be taped to the wall, but if it is possible to use drawing pins these are usually more successful. Each picture should be glued on to the required carton and the carton fastened on to the wall in the correct position. Once covered the cartons can be kept and used again for other friezes.

A suggestion for one year's art work

The following idea is not very original but has been used with much success in all classes. The basic picture contains a tree and a house linked by fringed, green crêpe paper to represent grass and blue sugar paper for the sky. The additional pictures should be fastened with drawing pins so that the whole frieze will not be spoilt with sticky tape.

Spring
Blossom on the tree can be represented by pink tissue paper. Each child can make daffodils, crocus and lambs. Chickens and bunnies can be added towards Easter. A bird's nest can be added to the chimney of the house, and maybe even a stork could be put on the nest.

Summer
Green leaves can be painted to replace the pink blossom on the tree. Sunflowers and daisies replace daffodils; a fieldmouse, horse or cow could substitute the Spring animals; some children could also be represented playing with a kite. Butterflies and bees make attractive mobiles if they are hung in front of the picture, and a sunbather could also be placed in front of the house.

Autumn
Actual dried and pressed leaves, or leaf prints, can be pinned to the branches of the tree, some on the grass and some 'falling' down. Each child could make a squirrel or an owl to sit in the tree, or a badger to lie in the grass. At Hallowe'en, a witch can be added 'flying' through the air on her broomstick. Towards November, a Guy Fawkes, bonfire and fireworks bring added vitality to the scene.

Winter
All the leaves should be removed from the tree and the branches left bare, or cotton-wool added to represent snow. One child could make a Bambi or reindeer perhaps, while others contribute to pictures of children on a sledge or skating on a pond. Towards Christmas, the scene can become a fantasy with fairies, dwarfs, pixies and Father Christmas, or it can be more traditional, having a stable, shepherds, kings and one single star in the sky. This latter scene is particularly effective if black silhouettes are used.

One year is quite sufficient for this long-term display. It not only starts to look worn, but the teacher and class become rather tired of the house and tree over twelve months.

A good display is essential in order to bring out the best in every picture. In fact, it is as important as the picture itself.

4 Cookery

Cookery plays a very important part in the timetable of the Special School, as every session leads the child a little closer to independence. Even if he can only make tea and toast, or sweep the floor clean, these regular household tasks will give him added interests in life and introduce him to a wider scope of experiences. The younger child needs to explore the realms of cooking, cleaning and washing, yet he may not want to take an active part in the actual cookery session but may simply enjoy watching the teacher make a cake. No doubt he will like to wash beakers after milk and wash clothes during water play. He should also have the opportunity to play with a mixture – getting sticky fingers and feeling it bind together is a lovely experience, especially for the partially sighted. Pastry play or dough play is well known in classrooms and often the child can put what he bakes into the oven. Baked slowly until it is very hard, it can be used as a 'cake' during shop play. It is also a good exercise for the younger child to learn about the cooker – that it is dangerous and can burn, but if used properly he has no need to fear it.

Cleanliness is of paramount importance and it is a good idea to encourage each child to wash his hands in the classroom, if possible, or go with him to the washroom, so that the teacher can make certain his hands are properly washed.

The older child must be expected to take a more serious interest in cookery, and have a positive aim in view. He should be taken frequently into supermarkets or hypermarkets (not on busy days) and taught to recognize various tins and packets of food. If possible he must be taught to discriminate between pet foods and tinned meat. Shopping cards can be made from many labels and packets, and if the price is printed on the card he should learn numbers too. (Decimalization is much easier, from the mentally handicapped child's point of view, than the old £.s.d.) If the child is to eat his cooking in school, as he may like to do, then he should learn the art of table-setting, using a tablecloth (or making his own mats), salt and pepper, knives, forks and spoons, and generally making the table look attractive and tidy. The teacher should aim for more self-sufficiency and the child should be taught everyday tasks like making toast, tea and coffee, and opening tins and packets of food. A very high ideal is for the most senior class – or each child with high potential – to be taught how to cook a meal of his own, but a great deal of time needs to be spent planning such an ambitious project. Convenience foods are probably the easiest to use. Fresh vegetables take so long to prepare, particularly as each child takes an active part, and the school day would be over before they were cooked. However, convenience foods do sometimes prove rather expensive, and there is still a great deal of weighing, measuring and reading involved. It is necessary for the school to establish whether the advantages of one outweigh the disadvantages of the other. Perhaps the class should be taught individual basic skills first, like making custard, instant mashed potatoes, frying fish fingers, hamburgers, mixing instant desserts and opening tins! After a year or so of hard work the class may eventually be able to cook a relatively simple meal for themselves. Undoubtedly the child who is encouraged daily to help at home will be much more capable of working in school.

Cookery sessions take quite a long time to organize and are often finished more quickly than expected. One of the main difficulties is to retain the interest of each child while teaching one or two individually. If, for example while mixing a cake, the teacher may be teaching the whole class, but it is only convenient for two to take an active part, the cookery charts the teacher may have made are not enough to retain the interest of the remainder of the class. One solution is for each child to be provided with his own small bowl and for the teacher to divide up the ingredients among the class. For example, if making pastry, each child could be given 1 oz flour and $\frac{1}{2}$ oz lard and shown how to 'rub in' the mixture. In this situation the child has something of his own to do whilst the teacher is able to take time with an individual child and teach him the rudiments of baking.

If an assistant is available, alternative solutions are possible. The teacher could take a small group, separately, while the remainder of the class works with the assistant; or the class could be split into two, with the assistant and the teacher teaching different cookery skills to each group. The groups could change over during the lesson. It is known from experience that the smaller the group the easier it is to teach and the more each child learns.

Below are lists of foods found to be suitable for cookery sessions with all ages. Some need cooking whilst others do not. It is hoped that most of the ideas are fairly economical and simple to prepare.

Many of the children like to take their cookery home and margarine pots are often suitable containers. Each child could have his own pot with his name on, and be encouraged to return it, washed, ready for use next time.

Uncooked ideas

Sandwiches (all ages – youngest need help)
Use slimmers' bread, or half a slice of ordinary bread as ESNs have a tendency to overweight. A sharp knife is essential to cut the bread, or pastry cutters can be used for fancy shapes for parties. Open sandwiches look more attractive and soft margarine is recommended for easier spreading.

Spreads (can be used on crackers too)

meat/fish paste	luncheon meat
cheese spread (no margarine needed); tubes are cheapest	sardines – sild cheaper?
	Marmite
cheese slices	peanut butter (no margarine needed)
pâté (expensive)	
sliced tomato, cucumber, banana	jam
	egg and cress (grow cress in class)

Fruit (all ages)
This is very attractive for summer cookery sessions as well as being good for diets. Every child will be interested in and like to taste sweet fruits, and it is a new experience for the very young or Special Care child to taste bitter or sour fruits. It is also interesting for the older child to compare the looks and flavour of tinned fruits with fresh or dried. All stones and pips can be planted in class (see Chapter 5: Nature).

It is often surprising how few ESNs children can peel a banana or orange, how many eat the core of an apple and indeed ask to have it peeled first!

Sweet	*Sour*	*Tinned*	*Dried*
apple	lemon	mandarin	raisins
orange	grapefruit	oranges	sultanas
banana	baking apple	apricots	currants

pear	some grapes	pineapple	dates
cherry	lime	rhubarb	prunes
grape	some plums	prunes	apricots
plum	apricot	fruit cocktail	figs
pineapple		pears	
melon		plums	
tomato		cherries	

Never eat rhubarb raw!
What happens to apples, bananas when left without peel?

Vegetables (all ages)

These are not as interesting as fruit, but can nevertheless be enjoyed in a number of ways. Visit a market garden or allotment or grow some easy vegetables in school (see Chapter 5: Nature). Some vegetables have skins which need to be peeled off, others have leaves. A few can be eaten raw, but are improved with slight cooking, and the colours are almost as varied as the colours of fruit. Several can be used raw in a salad.

Leafy vegetables	*Root vegetables*	*Bulbous vegetables*
cabbage	potato	onion
lettuce	carrot	spring onion
cauliflower	turnip	leek
broccoli	parsnip	shallot
purple-sprouting	swede	
broccoli	radish	
sprouts	beetroot	
spinach		

Unusual vegetables	*Various other vegetables*
red pepper	mushroom
green pepper	celery
courgette	parsley
aubergine	marrow
artichoke	cucumber
	cress
	peas
	beans

Ingredients for salad (5–16 years: all ages who can chew well)

lettuce	grated carrot
eggs	diced, cooked potato

tomatoes	parsley
cucumber	watercress
beetroot	peas
radishes	beans
celery	spring onion
cauliflower florets (raw)	onion rings
shredded cabbage (raw)	coleslaw, slimmer's salad
grated apple	cream

Fruit in a salad is pleasant too: apple, banana, tinned oranges, peeled grapes.

Any of the above can be used in a salad, though preferably not all at once!

Sweet making (7–16 years)
This should be regarded as a special treat for cookery sessions – at a party or the end of term, for example; or the older child could take some to a Special Care child to involve him in the activity.

Very simple marzipan sweets
Buy block marzipan, roll into balls, or cut into fancy shapes. Some marzipan can be coloured with food colouring – pink, green, etc.

Cherry sweet – Push chopped cherry into marzipan.

Nutty sweet – Roll marzipan in chopped nuts.

Minty sweet – Add peppermint essence to marzipan (colour green).

Chocolate sweet – Dip marzipan into melted chocolate
or
roll marzipan into chocolate vermicelli.

Toffee Crisps (all ages)
4 oz cream caramels
4 oz marshmallows
3 oz *Rice Krispies*
2 oz butter
Melt butter, caramels and marshmallows gently in large pan. When they have melted, stir in *Rice Krispies*. Press into square tin and leave to set. Cut into small squares.

No-bake cakes

Truffles – makes 16–18 (all ages)

4 oz stale cake crumbs
4 oz castor sugar
4 oz ground almonds
a little seedless jam
almond, rum, brandy, or sherry flavouring essence if liked
chocolate vermicelli

Crumble cake thoroughly (roll rolling-pin over crumbs). Mix all ingredients, except chocolate vermicelli, until well bound together. Form into small balls and leave to become firm. Cover each ball with little jam and roll in vermicelli.

Packet Cheesecake or *Simple Cheesecake* (7–16 years)

Flan case	10 digestive biscuits, crushed	blend together and line
	2 oz melted margarine	a flan case.
Filling	1 lemon jelly, cut up	Make up in basin.
	lemon juice	Reheat in pan if jelly
	$^1/_4$ pt boiling water	does not dissolve.
	8 oz cottage cheese *or*	
	8 oz *Philadelphia* cream cheese	
	4 oz double cream *or*	
	Dream Topping and milk	

When the jelly is nearly set whisk in the cheese. Place in fridge until nearly set (only about 5 minutes). Whisk in cream or *Dream Topping*. Spoon filling into flan case. Decorate with chocolate curls or other suitable decoration.

Quick summer desserts (all ages)

Sweetheart Desserts
jelly and ice cream
jelly and *Dream Topping*
jelly and fruit
bananas and evaporated milk
Angel Delight
Caramello
Royal Egg Custard (omit pastry
    case)
Royal Lemon Meringue Pie
    (omit pie and meringue, add
    slices of banana)
Birds Trifle

Instant Whip
Heinz Tinned Desserts
ice cream and fruit
fresh fruit salad
tinned fruit salad

} saucepan and hotplate
    required

Cooked ideas (all ages)

Toast

Use slimmers' bread again – toast only one side to prevent bread becoming hard, or use half a slice per child of ordinary bread – calorific value is approximately the same.

Toppings for toast
cheese slices
baked beans
grated cheese
scrambled eggs
sliced tomatoes

spaghetti
Heinz Toast Toppers
Crosse & Blackwell Hot Toast
   Savouries
Chesswood mushrooms

Recipe for mushrooms on toast
$^1/_2$ lb mushrooms, sliced
$^1/_2$ oz margarine (optional)
1 oz cornflour
salt and pepper
$^3/_4$ pint milk

Simmer the sliced mushrooms in the milk until they are tender. Mix the cornflour and seasonings with a little cold water or milk and add to simmering milk. Bring to the boil, stirring constantly. The margarine added at this stage gives the sauce a smoother consistency. Keep the sauce hot, but do not overcook whilst making the toast.

Soups (all ages)

Not a very exciting cookery lesson, but simple enough for each child to learn how to make some for himself, in case he ever needs to. It is good to compare ways of making soup, and interesting if more unusual varieties are chosen.

Unusual varieties
asparagus
chicken noodle
celery
lentil

Different types
ordinary, tinned
packets – require water
boxes – require water
tinned, condensed – require
   water or milk
instant – require boiling water

For 1-pint quantities a milk bottle can be used – for condensed soup use the can as a measure.

Eggs (all ages)
Children generally love eggs and they can be eaten in various ways. It is very nice to be able to supply one egg per child, but this isn't always practical, even if the smallest eggs are bought. Not many recipes can be taken home.

Ideas using one egg per child
1   Soft-boiled. A little vinegar in the water prevents the pan from staining.
2   Hard-boiled. Paint and decorate the shell for Easter, then take home.
3   Poached (on toast). A little lemon juice in the water helps the egg bind together if a poacher isn't available.

Ideas using half an egg (or less) per child (7–16 years)
1   Scrambled (on toast). Mix with milk for larger quantity.
2   Hard-boiled. Chopped up and mixed with cress for sandwiches.
3   Pancakes, omelettes. Not recommended, except possibly for senior classes.
4   Egg, onion and tomato (on toast). See recipe below.
5   Stuffed eggs. Hard-boil, cut in half, mix yolk with cottage cheese, replace yolk mixture. Take slice off the bottom of each egg half to make it stand up. Decorate with parsley, or paprika pepper.

Egg, onion and tomato
2 onions
6 medium tomatoes
6 eggs, beaten
seasoning
Peel, chop, gently fry onions in deep pan. Dip tomatoes in boiling water for a few seconds, remove and skin them (not absolutely necessary). When the onions are soft, slice the tomatoes and add to the onions. Add the eggs and cook gently for 4 minutes. Can be served on toast.

Cakes, scones, biscuits (all ages)
The easiest and sometimes the cheapest way is to use ready-to-mix packs of cakes. Usually it is only necessary to add an egg or milk, or even water. There is no need to weigh or measure so many different ingredients, although this can detract from the excitement of baking. Gingerbread Men are very popular with all ages, and sometimes it is

easier for the teacher to make the dough at home, so that each child will have time to make his own Gingerbread Man. It will be easier if the teacher can take each child individually, particularly in the case of the younger child.

Gingerbread Men (all ages – youngest with help)
12 oz flour
1 teasp. bicarbonate of soda
2 level teasp. ground ginger
4 oz butter/margarine
6 oz brown sugar
3 oz syrup (weigh the tin, remove 3 oz syrup)
1 egg, beaten
currants

Sift dry ingredients and rub in fat. Add the sugar. Warm syrup and egg and make dough. If no cutters are available then each child needs to roll one small ball, flattened out, for the head, a larger one for the body and four limbs. Each Gingerbread Man needs 3 currant buttons, 2 eyes, 1 nose and 3 currants for a mouth. Bake in a fairly hot oven (375°F, Gas Mark 5) for 10–15 minutes.

Swiss tarts (7–16 years)
4 oz margarine
1 oz sugar
vanilla essence
4 oz flour
seedless jam or jelly

Beat margarine and sugar together. When smooth add essence. Fold flour into mixture. Use a finger to press down blobs of the mixture into bun cases, making a well in the centre of each. Bake in medium oven (350°F, Gas Mark 4) for 20–25 minutes. When cold spoon a little jam in centre of each tart.

Flapjacks (7–16 years)
3 oz butter
3 oz brown sugar
4 oz porridge oats

Cream butter, gradually add other ingredients. Press evenly into square tin and bake in centre of hot oven (425°F, Gas Mark 7) for 15 minutes. Cool and cut into slices or squares.

Shortbread (7–16 years)
4 oz margarine
4 oz sugar
4 oz flour
2 oz ground rice
Cream together margarine and sugar. Add flour and rice, mix well. Press into square or round shallow tin, bake for 30–40 minutes in moderate oven (350°F, Gas Mark 4). Leave to cool and cut into slices or wedges.

Scones (10–16 years)
8 oz S.R. flour
1 teasp. baking powder
salt
1½ oz margarine
1½ oz sugar
2 oz currants
¼ pint milk
Rub fat into flour, baking powder and salt. Stir in sugar and fruit. Slowly add the milk. When mixture resembles smooth, soft dough, turn it out on to a floured surface. Roll out until it is about 1" thick. Cut with pastry cutter. Place on greased baking tray and bake near the top of a hot oven (450°F, Gas Mark 8) for 10 minutes.

Variations
Treacle scones: Add 1 tablespoon black treacle and 1 teaspoon mixed spice to above ingredients.
Sultana scones: Add sultanas in place of currants.
Raisin scones: Add raisins in place of currants.
Cheese scones: Omit sugar and add cheese in place of currants.

Dough for playtime (up to 10 years, including Special Care)
16 oz flour
4 oz salt
cooking oil to bind
any food colouring
The above ingredients provide a very elastic dough, which can be played with repeatedly. The salt prevents the mixture becoming mouldy and the cooking oil keeps it smooth. The mixture should be kept in a polythene bag when not in use.

Dough for 'pretend' cakes (all ages)
16 oz flour
8 oz salt
water to bind
Both the teacher and the child can make 'pretend' cakes for shop play. The dough must be kneaded well before it is baked. Many fancy breads and meat pies can be fashioned out of this dough. It has to be baked very slowly for a very long time until the 'cakes' are rock hard. 'Jam tarts' do not take quite so long because the dough is thinner, and the centre of these can be painted later with either yellow (lemon cheese) or red (jam) paint. The illusion of having 'real' cakes in the shop can be increased if the cakes are varnished when they are absolutely cold.

5 Nature

Few ESNs schools actually include nature on their timetable, yet it is important, particularly if the school is situated in a large metropolis, and the child can only see the countryside on rare occasions. Very often the parents of an ESNs child will not take him into the countryside, as they would a normal child. They may be ashamed that he is mentally handicapped and hide him away, or they may want to protect him to such a degree that he is not given the opportunity of rambling through woods, hills and dales in case he should fall and hurt himself. He is also very rarely permitted out on his own, or even with his brothers and sisters, so he is unable to explore local parkland thoroughly, as many normal children do. Therefore the teacher must bring some nature into the classroom for him. Each child needs to be encouraged to collect specimens for the nature table. He can collect from the school field at dinnertime, when out visiting a local park with his class, or when on a longer school trip to the seaside, lakes or woodland. It is through nature that the child learns about life, about pretty flowers, different animals and insects, sweetly-scented blossom in the spring, as well as the less pleasant farmyard smells – all this is nature and it should become a part of everyday life in the Special School.

It is good for the child to learn to cope with failure as well as success and he will discover that some seeds will grow easily, a few may never grow, while others wither and die as young seedlings. Extending this idea, the teacher can create some simple experiments within the classroom. Plants or seedlings can be kept without light or water and the results will prove how necessary sunshine and moisture are to all growing plants. The weekly nature session could involve planting seeds or pips, walking around the school grounds to find different flowers, or just removing every specimen from the nature table and discussing its properties, colour, shape and weight, for example. (This can be developed into a 'Bring-Me' game – see the section on Games in Chapter 7: Music.)

Almost every child will enjoy playing with the soil, it feels different to sand, clay and other mediums with which he is more familiar. A whole class could be given the opportunity of tidying up the school grounds, or even tend a small garden plot at regular intervals. It should not take long for one child, at least, to learn how to use a garden fork, trowel or rake, and this may well encourage the others, providing enough tools are available. Whatever the case, every child will probably enjoy pulling up the grass and weeds, hoping to find worms, beetles and other insects. It is entirely up to the teacher whether she encourages such a collection!

There are several other ways of bringing nature into the classroom. Many seeds, bulbs and pips can be grown successfully on the nature table, alongside non-growing things such as stones, shells, pine-cones and dead twigs. It is very useful to provide a large magnifying glass to observe these articles more closely. If possible, the teacher should grow indoor plants of various kinds which will not only be interesting for the child, but should also enhance the school as a whole, especially if they are placed in corridors and the entrance hall for all the staff and visitors to enjoy. During holiday periods, if it is not possible for the plants to be taken home, they should be removed from direct sun and placed in bowls of water, or stood in a bath full of wet newspaper. If possible the teacher should make a little time to look at the plants during the holiday, to ensure they are kept moist.

Every child seems to be fascinated by animals and insects too – and the class should be taken frequently on visits which enable them to observe these creatures close at hand. In addition to farms and zoos, which are obviously interesting visits, certain museums may have stuffed animals, moths and beautiful butterflies on display in glass cases. They may even have skeletons of large animals which will capture the child's imagination. A good fishmonger's or local fish market can also be of interest to the child. He would be able to see crab, lobster, conger-eel, whelks, shrimps and many other fascinating seafoods while the partially-sighted should derive some benefit from this kind of visit as the smell of fish is quite unique!

A great deal of careful thought is needed if pets are to be kept in school. Tropical fish are probably the most practical as they need very little attention during holiday periods. However, small mammals like mice and gerbils are a good deal more interesting, and the child can learn to handle such pets, providing the teacher ensures that each child takes great care, and treats the animal gently.

On the following pages are ideas which involve nature, both within the classroom and outside. They deal with many natural items to touch, smell, enjoy or simply examine – whether they are alive, moving and growing, or inflexible and dead. The teacher is by no means expected to provide all items at once, but should rearrange them on the nature table at regular intervals to stimulate and encourage each child to develop a more active interest in nature.

Plant life – inside (all ages)
Even if the child is too young or handicapped actually to plant seeds and bulbs, he can be encouraged to handle such things as stones, pine-cones and feathers, and can be shown the flowers and plants in the classroom, which itself will be considerably brightened with the presence of a nature table. This will be especially so if vases of flowers are displayed – like a few daffodils in the spring or some sweetly-scented roses during the summer.

Plain garden soil is adequate for many seedlings but a proprietary potting compost should produce healthier plants. Indoor plant food used regularly in the summer months will also ensure healthier growth.

Fruit (7–16 years)
   Pips and seeds
   Collect and label all pips.

orange	pear
apple	melon
grape	tomato
grapefruit	lemon

Dry out for 24 hours. Plant in soil – bury $^1/_2$" deep, keep moist.

Stones (5–16 years)

plum		date
peach	remove hard	cherry
damson	outer shell before	
prune	planting	
apricot		

Soak 24 hours before planting. Bury $1–1^1/_2$" deep in soil. Keep moist.

Special fruit (5–16 years)
Avocado
Remove brown skin from stone. Place round base over jar of water. (Use cocktail sticks pushed through stone to help balance if necessary.) Plant in soil when tap root is 3" long. (If planted directly into soil it takes several months to grow.)

Peanut
Shell monkey-nuts. Plant 1" deep in damp soil, keeping warm and moist. (Proper peanut plants produce pods above ground which bend over and ripen underground – it is unlikely these will develop so far.)

Pineapple
Slice top off pineapple. Scoop remaining fruit out of top. Dry out for 24 hours. Plant in damp soil – beware of overwatering until new growth becomes obvious. Fruiting may occur after 18 months – 2 years. (Always choose pineapple with green leaves.)

Vegetables (all ages)
Growing shoots

carrot turnip beetroot swede parsnip	Slice off tops and place them in saucer of water. Shoots will quickly grow. Carrots are pretty, fern-like, while beetroot shoots are very colourful.
potato	Choose old potato and leave to develop shoots.
mobile carrot	Choose large, firm carrot and slice $1/2$" off narrow end. Hollow out carrot with vegetable peeler. Hang upside-down above the nature table and fill with water. Shoots grow down first, then turn and grow upwards.

Growing roots (all ages)

leek onion shallot spring onion	Place base over jar of water, roots grow into the water. Shoots may grow upwards. Strong smelling.
potato	Place old potato in jar of water. Roots grow into water.

Growing roots and shoots (10–16 years)
Use dried vegetables, e.g.: butter beans, kidney beans, peas, black-eyed peas.
Place blotting paper around inside edge of jam jar. Push pea/bean in between jar and paper. Fill jar with wet sand – do not allow to dry out. Shoots and roots grow from peas and beans.
Experiment: Keep some dry and some dark.

Experiment with celery (all ages)
Place sticks of celery into jar of coloured water – water will be seen to rise up celery.

Seeds (10–16 years)
Many flowers and plants are easily grown from seed – some are even edible. Flowers with large or pelleted seeds are easy for each child to plant one or two of his own.

Scented, pretty flowers	*Edible plants*
nasturtium	mustard and cress
marigold (calendula)	alfalfa (tastes like peas)
sweet pea	tomato (full sun needed to fruit)

Bulbs (all ages)
Bulbs, too, are easy to grow and produce very attractive flowers in the Spring. The bulb fibre needs to be well soaked for at least twenty-four hours before use and several bulbs planted close together provide a more effective display than single ones. However, if every child wishes to plant his bulb in a separate pot, then yoghurt cartons are quite suitable for the small bulbs. After planting, keep the bulbs in a cool, dark place with no further watering until the shoots appear. Do not bring into daylight until the shoots are about 3" long and water frequently. Planting time: September to October for flowering December, January, February.

Large bulbs	
daffodil	tulip
narcissus	hyacinth (blue, very sweetly scented)

Plant with tops of bulbs slightly protruding above soil.

Smaller bulbs	
crocus	iris reticulata
snowdrop	bluebell (Scilla)
glory of the snow (Chionodoxa)	grape hyacinth (Muscari)

Bury bulbs $1-2^1/_2$" deep, depending on bulb size (i.e. larger bulbs buried deeper).

Individual teaching using pre-reading apparatus which involves (*right*) matching pictures to pictures and (*below*) matching words to pictures and letters to words (page 156)

wing is a practical activity which
ds good coordination and helps to
velop fine motor control (page 81)

Learning to swim with the teacher giving physical support (page 125)

Towards independence: a senior group learn to prepare their own dinner (page 49)

The climbing frame develops muscle contr confidence and imagination (page 12c

Also try smaller flowering varieties of:

daffodil
narcissus
tulip (some have pretty, dark, spotted leaves)
autumn crocus – plant June, July to flower October, November

Consult seed catalogues and bulb specialists for further reference or buy from large store/garden centre which has a good selection of seeds and bulbs. Always take note of planting instructions on the back of packets.

Indoor plants
Most of the following have been selected for their interesting habits or flowers, and all are very easy to grow. Most are best if they are bought as plants, though they can be raised from cuttings, seeds or corms.

Climbing or trailing
Ivy
Many varieties – variegated, small-leaved and sharp-edged most interesting. Natural habit to trail, but can be trained to climb.
Tradescantia (Wandering Jew)
Very easy to grow. Cuttings easy to propagate. Various colours, purple/green stripes, some have small pink flowers. Always grown as trailing plant.
Geranium
Ivy-leaved variety trails, with pale pink flowers on long stems. Rests in winter.
Spider-plant or Striped Grass
Not strictly trailing but has 'baby plants' which trail. Pale green spiky leaves with light stripe. Very easy to grow.
Philodendron (Sweetheart plant)
Thick heart-shaped dark green leaves. Usually grown as climber. Has stubby aerial roots.
Passion-flower
Beautiful flowers, white/blue, which last twenty-four hours only. Needs full sun to flower. Usually grown as climber. Very vigorous. Re-pot as soon as roots seen through base of pot. Cut stem right down in March. Feed regularly.

Foliage plants
Fatsia Japonica (Castor-oil plant)

Easy to grow. Has large, glossy, interesting leaves, deeply cut, palmate. Variegated form available.

Rubber-plant

Easy to grow. Can become very tall. New leaves red before opening out.

Begonia

Many varieties. 'Rex' is best known of foliage begonias (fan plant). Pink and green markings on leaves. Grows well once established.

Coleus

Annual only. Can be grown from seed. Many colours and patterns on sharply-toothed leaves. Variety of nettle, but does not sting. Remove flower heads to prevent plant becoming leggy.

Monstera (Swiss-cheese plant)

Holes in leaves fascinate child. Also has aerial roots growing out from stem. Growth increased if these are packed with damp moss.

Venus's fly-trap

Catches flies and fascinates child. Full sun is required for bright red colour in 'traps'. Grow in sphagnum moss.

Staghorn-fern

Interesting as no plant pot is required. Grows on bark padded with sphagnum moss and kept moist.

It is useful to note that the foliage of all the above-mentioned plants can be damaged if the plants are placed in a sunny position behind frosted or opaque glass.

Flowering plants

Primula

Many attractive varieties. Clumps of flowers grow at the top of tall stems. Many colours – yellow, pink, purple. Annual, but can be kept longer; flowers anytime.

Geranium

Very bright red flowers on tall stems. Needs to rest in winter.

African violet

Pretty flowers in summer. Evergreen leaves. Needs moist atmosphere.

Begonia (Semperflorens is easiest and most popular variety)

Popular as bedding plant. Small flowers almost all year round. Cuttings easy to take. Choice of colours: flowers white, pink or red; leaves dark red or green.

Streptocarpus (Cape primrose)

More unusual but pretty and very easy to grow. Push a half-leaf into soil during June, July for flowering following year. Evergreen tall stems produce pink/purple/blue trumpet-like flowers during summer months.

Achimines (Hot-water plant)

Different again. Dark green/purple leaves grow 12–15" tall and produce many blue/purple flowers all the way up. Dry out in winter. Split tiny corms and re-pot in February/March. Water well and liquid feed throughout summer. Cease watering in October.

Bottle gardens

Bottle gardens should really only be attempted by the ambitious. It is unlikely that any child will be capable of making one of these, but they are very interesting for him to examine as well as being decorative for the school. Never choose plants which are vigorous growers – they get out of hand in a restricted container. Coarse gravel and charcoal should be placed in the bottom of the jar for well-drained, cleaner conditions, and then potting-compost mixed with sand added. The bottle may be horizontal or upright, but landscape the plants first outside the bottle as it is difficult to rearrange them once they are inside. It will be easier to manipulate the plants into position using spoons, forks and wooden cotton-reels attached to long sticks which will reach the base of the bottle. Once watered, the plants will settle in and probably not require further watering for several months.

Suitable plants

Begonia – choose the smaller-leaved variety.

Spider-plant – thin leaves spread out to make an attractive background.

Maranta (arrowroot) – very attractive green/purple foliage with stripes.

Peperomia – light-coloured veins on dark leaves – almost corrugated appearance.

Pilea (Aluminium plant) – dark green leaves with silvery patches between leaves.

Sansevieria (Mother-in-law's tongue) – attractive centrepiece in tall bottle.

Moss, rocks, pebbles and shells can also be added to make it like a miniature garden.

Plants for the partially-sighted

There are very few 'house plants' which are particularly suitable for this child, but many garden flowers and herbs can be displayed either as pot-plants or cut flowers in vases for him to smell, taste and feel.

Herbs (aromatic and distinctive to taste)

mint	lavender
chives (like onions)	rosemary
sage	thyme
lovage (like celery – grows 7–8 ft.)	parsley
	marjoram (like aniseed)

Flowers (aromatic)

geranium (ordinary/mint scented/lemon scented)	catmint (Nepeta)
	hyacinth
marigold (Calendula)	lilac
nasturtium	honeysuckle
sweet pea	lily of the valley
rose	stocks

Garden plants

Prickly	*Soft*
holly	pussy-willow catkins
sea-holly	pampas grass (seedhead)
rose	lambs tongues (stachys lanata) (non-flowering light grey leaf, feels like velvet)
berberis	
teasel	
cactus	*Sticky*
pines	petunia
conifers	horse-chestnut bud ('sticky-bud' becomes furry on opening)
pampas grass (leaf very sharp)	
	sun-dew insectivorous plant

Plant life – outside

This section is simply a list of items which could be collected on visits and brought back for display on the nature table as a reminder. Not all are strictly in the category of plant life, but nevertheless they are useful to the teacher who is constantly endeavouring to acquire a varied selection of natural articles for a good classroom display.

Woodland
The following can be displayed on a bed of leaves or moss:

Acorns – with and without shell.
Conkers – with and without prickly shell.
Sycamore seeds ('wings') – plant some, and grow trees!
Bark – rough, smooth, light, dark.
Pine-cones – different shapes, sizes. Keep some dry, some in water. Look for some part-eaten by squirrels.
Moss – collect different sorts – keep moist in saucer of water, or find stones covered with moss.
Mould and fungi – DO NOT COLLECT – CHILD MAY BE TEMPTED TO EAT. Instead grow mould on bread or fruit in the classroom.
Bird's nest – DO NOT ENCOURAGE CHILD TO COLLECT – he will not understand when it can be collected and may disturb eggs or fledglings.
Feathers – many ordinary feathers easily found. Ask Pets' Corner Warden or Zoo Keeper for more unusual feathers. Buy peacock's feather from local market.
Burrs – from burdock; small hooks fasten burrs onto clothing or fur.
Leaves – all shapes, colours and sizes – most attractive during Autumn.

Seashore
Display on a bed of sand:

Driftwood – look for interesting shapes, light and dark wood, heavy and light.
Shells – look for biggest, smallest; hinged scallops or razor shells, whelks, snails and spiny ones.
Seaweed – find green thick, thin or brown and bladder-wrack with air bubbles to pop!
Stones – look for stripes, speckles, smooth, rough and encrusted with barnacles. Keep some in water to change colour.
Crabs – dead crabs or shrimps will be of interest to the child, but shouldn't be kept long as they have a tendency to smell nasty. (Look for hermit crabs, but do not collect.)
Sea-holly – prickly plant.
Thrift (sea pink) – clusters of pink flowers on tall stems grow from mound of 'grass'.
Whelk egg case – very light in weight, brown clusters of holes.

Grasslands
Display on a bed of moss or bracken:

Grasses – many different varieties, tall or short, with and without seedheads.

Oats, barley, wheat – child not expected to identify individual cereals.

Bullrush – take care when collecting – tends to grow in marshy ground.

Wild flowers – heather, dandelion, buttercup, daisy, clover (four-leaved – lucky!), gorse, bluebell, foxglove, willow-herb, etc.

Bracken, ferns – tall, fresh and green or brown and dead.

Preserving flowers
Method 1 – pressing
Carefully open flower out and dry flat between tissue-paper in pages of heavy book.
Method 2 – silica-gel
Preserve more colour by carefully burying flower-heads in crystals of silica-gel for 3–4 days.
Method 3 – borax
As above, but use borax for 3–4 weeks. (Both silica-gel and borax are obtainable from chemists – but borax should be discarded after use, while silica-gel can be used many times.)
Method 4 – air drying
Some plants, e.g. heather, sea-holly, will dry well simply by hanging upside-down in a warm place.
Method 5 – glycerine
Use two parts hot water to one part glycerine for preserving leaves such as beech, which turn an attractive coppery colour. Stand stems in liquid for 2–3 weeks.

Animal life – inside
All classroom pets must be well cared for at all times especially during holiday periods. NO child should be relied upon to care enough on his own!

Birds

| budgerigar | canary |
| parrot | minah bird |

Think about noise distraction in the classroom – these are usually better kept in corridors or entrance hall.

Animals

gerbil	mouse
guinea pig	rabbit
hamster	tortoise

If keeping more than one, be prepared for multiplication!
Tortoise – hibernates 4–5 months during winter.

Insects

worms – can be kept in a wormery
stick insects – interesting, as hard to distinguish from branches of tree
Few other insects are easy to observe in the classroom, though they can be kept in improvised containers with soil and stones.

Aquatics

Tropical fish – easy to care for, no problem during holidays. Buy compatible fish, snails to keep the water clean and weeds to help oxygenate the water.

Terrapins – interesting tiny green animals resembling turtles. They like warm water and need stones protruding above surface to 'sunbathe'. They eat live insects, raw meat and breathe air. WARNING: TERRAPINS ARE CARRIERS OF THE SALMONELLA VIRUS.

Tadpoles – keep frogspawn until tadpoles are quite large – even starting to grow back legs, then return them to the pond. Few will survive to become frogs in the classroom – the 'home-made' indoor pond is not large enough and the tadpoles become carnivorous and eat each other.

More information for school pets can be obtained from *Pets for Children* by S. and K. Denham (Hamlyn All-Colour Paperbacks 1969).

Animal life – outside

Birds

There are many activities associated with observing birds outside in natural surroundings, and many ways in which a child can appreciate bird life. One child may learn the names of one or two different birds, another may want to feed them, while yet another may get enough pleasure by simply watching them. Below are lists of suitable activities, places to visit and finally the more common birds and their habitat.

Birdwatching activities
1 All ages:
    (a) Throw bread and other food scraps on nearest *raised* surface. (Grass is not suitable as this may encourage mice.) Take bread to park and feed ducks.
    (b) Provide water bath in summer.
    (c) Provide water for drinking, winter and summer.
    (d) Hang out line in spring containing fur, wool, cotton, straw, cloth, hair, twigs, leaves, etc. See which birds build nests first.
    (e) String together monkey-nuts in winter. (Plant some – see Special Fruit, this chapter). Hang up on nearest post.
2 7–16 years:
    (a) Provide half a coconut for blue tits. When finished re-fill empty shell with food scraps bound together with melted fat and hang upside down. *Warning: Do not use desiccated coconut – it swells up inside and can kill birds.*
    (b) Make bird table and use it.
3 10–16 years:
    (a) The ambitious could make a bird house (place in sheltered position).
    (b) Make a histogram to see which birds are seen most frequently from classroom windows.

More information about bird tables can be found in *The New Bird Table Book* by Tony Soper (Pan Paperback 1975).

Places to visit
Special trips:
    (a) Farne Islands Bird Sanctuary, Northumberland.
    (b) Birdland, Bourton-on-the-Water, Gloucestershire.
Any bird sanctuary:
    List available from Royal Society for the Protection of Birds (who will also be willing to answer any queries about bird life).

zoo	seaside
farm	park
pet shop	lake, canal or riverbank

Most common birds

Garden	Farm	Zoo	Waterside
sparrow	chicken	penguin	duck
robin	hen	flamingo	swan

blackbird	cockerel	peacock	moorhen
starling	rooster	eagle	seagull
thrush	goose	parrot	kingfisher
magpie		owl	
blue tit		emu	
pigeon		ostrich	
chaffinch			

Animals

Observing animals outside is not quite as easy as observing birds; relatively few can be seen in the wild and even fewer will come near the classroom to be seen. Listed below are interesting visits to observe animal life.

Places to visit
(a) Domestic:
   pets' corner
   seaside (donkeys on sand) } all ages
   pet shop
   farm
   kennels } 7–16 years
(b) Woodland and countryside:
   parkland (all ages)
   woodland (7–16 years)
   nature reserves
   nature trail } 10–16 years
   moorland
(c) Wild:
   zoo
   safari park
   museum (stuffed animals) } all ages
   marineland
   circus (7–16 years)

Insects

These can largely be divided into two categories – those which fly and those which crawl. In addition is the earthworm, which is not strictly an insect, nor does it fly or crawl, but each child will find worms fascinating and may well wish to handle them.

Flying	Crawling
bee	ant
wasp	beetle
butterfly	centipede
ladybird	earwig
fly	snail
bluebottle	slug
moth	spider
dragonfly	

Aquatic life

There are many interesting activities associated with water and, providing the teacher is fully aware of the danger involved and takes all the precautions necessary, a group can have a good deal of fun fishing for aquatic life.

Fresh water	Seaside	Fish to eat	Water's edge
frogspawn	crab	cod	frog
toadspawn	hermit-crab	kipper	toad
pond skater	prawn	salmon	newt
shrimp	sand-worms	trout	snail
goldfish	jellyfish	tuna	
stickleback	starfish	sardine	
'tiddlers'			

Aquatic activites

7–16 years:

(a) Make fishing jars, nets or rods, go fishing.

(b) Go rock-pooling (just look, don't catch anything).

5–10 years:

Wade in wellingtons (*not* muddy water – too dangerous).

Visits

trip on canal, lake, river, ferry, sea
fishmonger's shop
fishmarket
fishing port, village
fish farm
seaside
aquarium

6 Handicrafts

The word handicraft means manual skill which may sound ambitious for the ESNs child. However, it does not refer to intricate embroidery or woodcarving, but to the simple, pretty or useful items the mentally handicapped child may be able to make in school.

At one time handicrafts were almost the only activities taking place in junior training centres, but now that the mentally handicapped child is no longer regarded as 'ineducable', crafts take second place to more intellectual pursuits. However, they should not be totally neglected, for simple handicrafts benefit the child in many ways, and he will become a more independent member of society if he has learnt one or two basic crafts, like sewing on a button or joining two pieces of wood together with a hammer and nail.

Many parents and possibly even some teachers may be anxious about the child learning woodwork skills. They may worry that he will cut his finger or hurt his thumb, but if the woodwork session is well supervised and the child is taught to respect the tools and use them sensibly, then serious accidents are unlikely.

The teacher will have little time in one week to provide shellcraft, woodwork, needlecraft, as well as modelling sessions, but with careful planning she should be able to set aside one lesson a week for general crafts. She may wish to be formal and teach every child the same craft at the same time or she may prefer a more informal approach, teaching one group woodwork, whilst another makes jewellery and a third learns needlecraft. This can often be more successful, as one child may be talented at modelling, whilst another prefers creating patterns and designs. Similarly, a teacher who is talented in one particular craft herself should be able to develop each child's full potential in that craft. However, she must not expect too high a standard from the mentally handicapped child because he will not be critical of his own work, but will be proud of his smallest achievements. Many items he makes will probably be suitable as small presents for Christmas, Easter and other special occasions. It will give his parents pleasure and pride to know that their handicapped child is able to make small gifts for them.

As with every skill this child learns, he absorbs craft skills slowly. The first table games he masters often precede simple skills – for example, the reception class may have early threading apparatus like coloured balls to push on to sticks, or a stick to thread through holes in a block of wood. The child develops from using these simple pieces of apparatus to threading large beads, finally learning the delicate skill of threading a needle.

Many of these handicrafts extend different areas of development in the ESNs child. For example, the moulding and shaping of clay exercises his finger muscles and helps manipulation but it is unlikely that anything moulded from school clay by his inexpert hands and probably without the use of a kiln will resemble fine china. However, the child will be thrilled with it, particularly after he has painted and decorated it, and is able to take it home. Likewise, hammering a nail into wood demands accurate coordination between hands and eyes, but although his wooden creation is not going to be a masterpiece of precision joints, he will be proud of it and eagerly show it to his friends, staff and parents.

Few traditional crafts have been included in this book because most of them take too long to accomplish and require a very high standard of achievement. However, should the teacher herself be accomplished in the art of basketry or rushwork, for example, she may be able to teach the child the rudiments of such crafts. Some of the modern crafts, like simple nail and thread designs or plastic casting, may be a little easier or quicker to accomplish. However, in many of these specialized crafts, it will probably be more satisfactory to buy patterns and kits from handicraft shops, although obviously this will be a greater expense. Listed below are practical suggestions for simple handi-craft items the mentally handicapped child could make in school.

Modelling with clay (all ages)

Equipment

clay	button
posterpaint	*Lego* brick
polyurethane	wooden bead
varnish	metal bottle-top
	large safety-pin
	old jewellery

for impressing designs and patterns

There are many different types of clay on the market and the teacher would be well advised to find the one most suited to her needs. The younger ESNs child will probably only want to feel and play with the clay, so it would be best for his teacher to order the cheapest available. The older child, however, may well want to make a lasting model to take home. As it is unlikely that the school has a kiln for firing natural clay then one of the self-hardening clays such as *Cold Clay* may be more suitable.

Of the natural clays there are two colours available, grey and terracotta. The main problem with clay is that it dries and cracks rather quickly. When not in use, it should be stored in a polythene bag, preferably inside a closed bucket. After use, place the remaining clay in the bucket and make a well in the centre. Fill the well quarter full with water, close the bag and the bucket and store until required, preferably in a cool place.

Things to make (for display only – not to be used)

dish	paperweight
cup	'bird's egg'
vase	beads

Modelling with papier-mâché (10–16 years)

Equipment

For the papier-mâché
newspaper
coloured newsprint, e.g.
    football green or pink, or
    comic strips
white tissue-paper ⎫ or white
white toilet-paper ⎬ emulsion
                    ⎭ paint
cold-water paste,
    e.g. *Polycell*
paint
varnish

For the moulds
Vaseline (spread on mould for
    easier removal when
    papier-mâché is dry)
margarine pot
yoghurt pot
plastic milk bottle
plastic bottle
balloon
cardboard tube/sheet/card
egg-box cartons

There are several methods of making papier-mâché, but the easiest and possibly the cleanest is called laminated paperwork. It is quite a long process if correctly made, but there are a few short cuts which are satisfactory for the ESNs child. Instant papier-mâché is available from craft shops and is a grey powdery substance, which needs to be mixed with water. It has not been used very successfully as it cracks rather easily when it has dried.

The most important aspect of making laminated paperwork is to tear the newspaper up into tiny pieces – large pieces of newspaper will not make the finished model hard enough. Each piece of paper must be thoroughly soaked with cold-water paste, and then put on the model. It is not vital that the child waits for each layer to dry before covering it with another layer. However, if various colours of newsprint are used for each layer then it will be easier to see that the whole model is evenly covered. The final layer of white tissue or toilet-paper is simply an alternative to painting the model with white emulsion prior to decoration.

Things to make

vase
dish
maracas

mask
animal

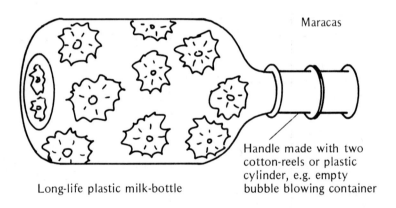

Maracas

Long-life plastic milk-bottle

Handle made with two cotton-reels or plastic cylinder, e.g. empty bubble blowing container

First ensure that the container is completely dry. Then quarter-fill it with sand. Join container and 'handle' parts together – remembering to block the holes in the cotton-reels first. Cover the whole model with papier-mâché. When it is completely dry, paint and decorate, then varnish.

Paper-bag mask
Stuff a large paper bag with newspaper until it is fairly hard. Cover one side with *Vaseline* and mark spaces for the eyes and mouth. Leaving these free, cover the *Vaseline* with papier-mâché to form

the basis of a mask. Keep adding the papier-mâché until the mask feels fairly solid. When it is dry, peel off the paper bag from the back and reinforce the eye and mouth holes with more papier-mâché. When the mask is completely dry, paint and decorate it, gluing wood shavings or wool on for hair.

An animal
Blow up a balloon, choosing the shape according to the kind of animal required. Spread *Vaseline* over the balloon and cover it with papier-mâché. If the animal requires a snout, cover a yoghurt pot in the same way. When the latter is dry remove the yoghurt pot and join the two parts together with more papier-mâché. When the whole is completely dry, push a pin through to pop the balloon. If liked egg-boxes or cardboard tubes can be used for legs. This basic shape can be used to make: a pig, a hedgehog, a 'sausage dog', or an elephant.

Modelling with wood (10–16 years)

Equipment

wood (offcuts available from building sites)
hammer
nails
carpet-tacks (large head, easier to hit)
screws
screwdriver
gimlet (helps to screw in screws)
strong glue (PVA adhesive or Evo-Stik)

sandpaper
hooks and eyelets (for joining pieces of wood to make a train)
saw (only to be used with strict supervision)
paint
varnish
wooden cotton-reels } useful as funnels and
metal bottle-tops } wheels

The teacher would be well advised to use well-sanded or polished wood, otherwise she may spend all her time removing splinters. The child will usually be able to make his own models once he is able to hammer a nail. He will not be able to saw or chisel accurate joints, but should be able to make a variety of simple items.

Things to make

boat
aeroplane
train

submarine
dolls' furniture
tray

paddlesteamer
teapot stand

Train

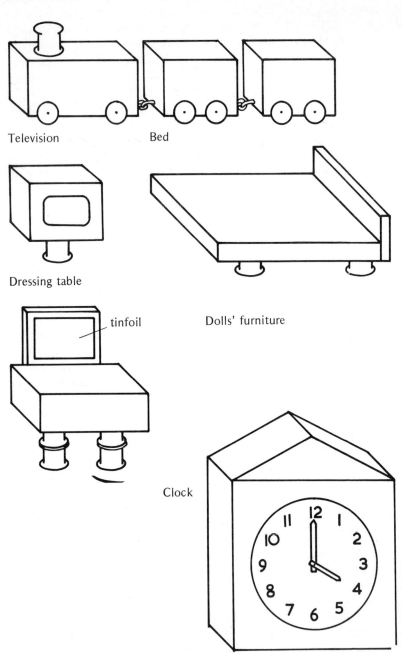

Television

Bed

Dressing table

tinfoil

Dolls' furniture

Clock

Paddle steamer

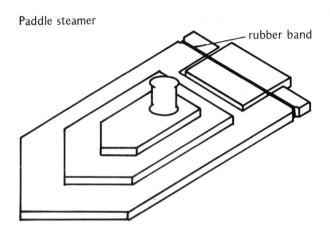

rubber band

Needlecraft (10–16 years)
The mentally handicapped child will feel a great sense of achievement and a useful member of the household if he has learnt to use a needle and thread. Yet sewing on a button is quite a complex task, and it is only the child with good eyesight and excellent control of his individual finger muscles who may be able to learn such a skill. Knitting, French knitting and embroidery are other skills which come under the general heading of needlecraft and each capable child should be encouraged to enjoy, and be shown how to make, the various stitches and patterns involved.

Embroidery is a particularly difficult skill to learn and if the teacher herself has a special aptitude for it and a child shows some talent in this direction, then he could be encouraged to use his talent and make a set of table-mats, showing three or four different stiches in bright decorative colours.

Equipment

large-eyed needle
assorted cottons, threads and wools
large-sized knitting needles

buttons, toggles
materials, e.g. loose-weaved canvas, felt
old stockings or tights (for padding)

Things to make
Felt fish (pin-cushion) (13–16 years)
Cut out basic fish shape on double material. Stitch pieces together, leaving front open. Turn fish inside out, stuff with old tights. Sew up front of fish. Sew on two buttons for eyes.

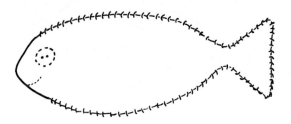

Sock puppet (13–16 years)
Find an old sock – preferably in a bright colour. Sew on two small buttons for eyes and a small piece of red felt for a tongue. If wished, ears can be added (soft brown felt for floppy ears, or stiff card painted pink on one side to represent donkey's or rabbit's ears). Add assorted materials for a more interesting face: for example, shoe-lace eyebrows and whiskers made of waxed dental floss, which is available from chemists.

Snuggy snake (10–16 years)

This is a very popular kind of draught excluder, which rests behind doors. Cut two pieces of material 3–4 ft long and about 18" wide. Sew the material together until it is 6" from the end, turn inside-out and stuff the snake with old tights. When it's nearly full fold the two raw edges inwards and neatly sew. Sew on a small piece of red felt for the tongue and two buttons for eyes.

Scented bag (7–16 years)

This is a popular gift on Mother's Day. Choose some brightly-coloured cotton material and cut it in a circle 18" in diameter. Hem the edge of the material and then gather it together with ribbon. Put a clean margarine-pot lid or round cheesebox lid in the bag to make a base. Fill the bag with rose petals or crushed herbs like lavender, thyme or rosemary. Pull the ribbon tightly and tie the ends in a pretty bow.

Table mat (13–16 years)

A table mat is a useful decorative article which can demonstrate the child's first embroidery stitches. Loose-weaved canvas is necessary so that the child can clearly see where to push his needle and thread. On page 84 are examples of simple stitches.

Running Stitch

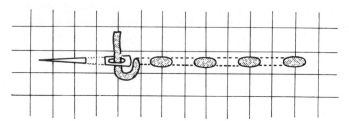

Laced Running Stitch

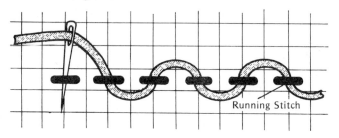

Running Stitch

Half Cross Stitch

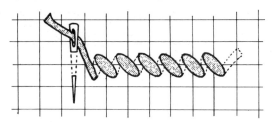

Satin Stitch

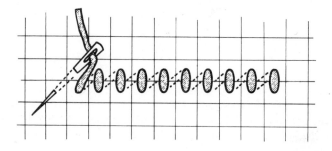

Diagonal Stitch

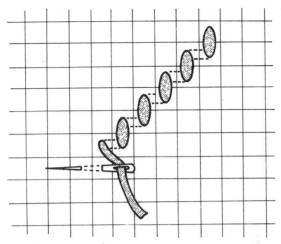

Woolly ball (7–16 years)

The younger child could probably make one of these without too much difficulty. The teacher needs to cut out two cardboard circles about 2–3" in diameter, each with a small circle cut out of the middle. The circles are put together and wool is wound around the cardboard, as in the diagram. When no more wool can be pushed through the hole, even with the help of a needle, then cut through the wool between the cards until all the strands are cut. Tie some wool around the centre of the ball and tightly knot it. Cut the cards into pieces and take them out of the woolly ball.

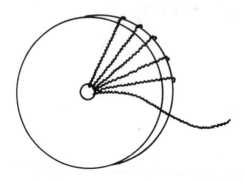

Knitting (13–16 years)

The teacher should provide large plastic or wooden knitting needles and some thick wool or string. The child probably only needs to be taught the basic knitting stitch and he will probably need a good deal of help at first, especially when casting on and off. If he shows an aptitude for knitting then he can be taught to make other patterns like stocking stitch which requires him to knit a row, purl a row. Very simple shapes are needed if the child is to make a whole article himself, for example:

a dishcloth from a square of knitted string
a doll's blanket from a square of knitted wool
a doll's scarf from a long piece of knitted wool.

French knitting (10–16 years)
For this simple activity the child needs an empty wooden cotton-reel with four small nails hammered in the top, some wool and a darning needle. To cast on, push one end of the wool down the centre hole and wrap the wool around each nail. Bring the loose end of the wool around the outside of each nail and, using the darning needle, pull the bottom loop over the top, working from one nail to the next in rotation. The knitted wool will appear through the bottom of the reel (see diagrams). The knitted wool can be used as braid for trimming articles or coiled round and round for individual mats or teapot stands.

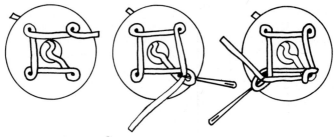

Simple weaving (10–16 years)
This is another relatively simple craft, but it is not as well known perhaps as French knitting. Its main use is decorative rather than useful, nevertheless it is good practice for the mentally handicapped child to learn patterns and a sequence of movements. Two sticks of equal length and an assortment of wool are all that is required.

Place the sticks together cross-wise and lash the wool around the centre of them in a figure of eight. Then wrap the wool around each stick in rotation, pulling the wool tight. When a new colour of wool is required simply knot the wool together and position the knot on the wrong side.

Decorative crafts

Making jewellery (7–16 years)
Most of the jewellery mentioned here involves threading something to make necklaces or bracelets; anything more superior such as coiling metal shapes for brooches is really too advanced for the ESNs child to create. Nevertheless, many attractive necklaces can be fashioned out of everyday items and all the child will need is some thread, a needle and seeds or beads for threading.

Threading necklaces and bracelets (7–16 years)
Suggested beads

washed, dried melon seeds
  (alternate with water-melon
  seeds)
wooden beads
plastic beads
pasta shapes
shells

clay beads
metal nuts and washers
sequins (very hard to thread –
  tiny hole)
buttons

Suggested threads
nylon thread (tough but slippery to knot)
cotton (not very tough)
shirring or hat elastic – various thicknesses
linen carpet thread – assorted colours

Paper beads (10–16 years)
These are quite easy to make with a thin knitting needle, some pages from a glossy magazine and glue.

Divide the magazine pages into rectangles approximately 3" by $\frac{1}{2}$" and cut every rectangle into two triangles. Cover the triangles with glue and roll around the knitting needle starting at the wide end and finishing with the narrow point of the triangle in the middle. Remove it from the knitting needle and leave to dry. Make several of these paper 'beads' and thread them with nylon or hat elastic.

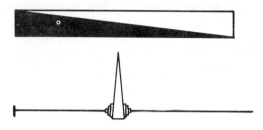

Chokers (10–16 years)

1 An attractive choker can be made from some $\frac{1}{2}$"–1" wide velvet ribbon and a fancy button. The child will only need to sew the button on and fix a press-stud fastener at the back.

2 Strips of dyed suede or leather could be plaited to make an unusual choker, and knotted or fastened with beads.

Shellcraft

Working with shells is an interesting craft, but the child needs a delicate touch as many shells, particularly the smaller ones, are quite brittle. Shells have many shapes and sizes and therefore can be joined together to make interesting figures like shell dolls or animals. Unfortunately, these days it is unusual to find really big shells or intricately-shaped shells on the shores around Britain. However, many decorative items can be created from the most ordinary cockles or mussels!

Equipment
assorted shells
PVA glue
Polyfilla
paint

polyurethane varnish
nail varnish
old containers, e.g. biscuit
   tins, cardboard boxes,
   plastic cartons

Things to make
Jewellery box (10–16 years)
Choose a suitably-sized carton or tin with a lid. The old fashioned

Christmas-time date-box is a good shape. Simply glue shells on the outside of the box, except where the lid is going to fit. Glue shells all over the lid. If liked, fill in the spaces with *Polyfilla*. The shells can be painted and varnished or decorated with pretty, pale colours of nail varnish.

Plant-pot holder or vase (all ages)

Use an empty plastic container as the basic shape for these pots, such as a large 1-lb margarine tub for the plant-pot holder and a wide-necked plastic bottle for the vase. Cover the outside of the containers with *Polyfilla* and embed the shells into it before it sets. Even the youngest child could manage to push a shell into the *Polyfilla*, and possibly paint it afterwards. The teacher will need to make sure that the *Polyfilla* is not too thin or it will not adhere to the pot.

Shell picture (10–16 years)

Shells can be used in any picture – as collage material on a seaside scene, for instance. However, they can also be made to look attractive as individual designs. A formal picture, like a bunch of flowers, could be fashioned from assorted shells, or the child could create an abstract design by grouping the shells in his own way. The shells should, however, be arranged into the decorative design first, and if they need to be painted then the child should paint the shells before gluing them into their final position. It is better to display them on card, because paper is too thin to take the weight of a lot of shells.

Shell figures – animals and people (13–16 years)

With the different shapes and sizes of shells many interesting and amusing figures can be made very simply and with a little imagination. For example, a bi-valve or clam could be a lady's skirt, a snail shell glued to it makes her head and a limpet serves as her hat! Tiny shells make good eyes and clams could be feet for the figures to stand firmly.

Tying and dyeing (10–16 years)

Equipment

cold-water dye	salt
plastic bowl	soda
string	

This is an ancient craft whereby old fabrics are rejuvenated. Currently it is undergoing restoration and tying and dyeing has become a very popular craft. There are two basic ways of dyeing material: using cold-water or hot-water dyes. Obviously the only practical method to use in the classroom is a cold-water dye, and this will only work on natural fabric such as cotton or linen. The basic method of tying and dyeing is to do just that – tie knots in the material and dye it! Salt and soda need to be added to the solution, but the instructions on the packet will list the amounts necessary. If each child is to tie and dye his own article then a handkerchief or something equally small would be suitable. The container used for the dyeing will probably have to be discarded after use, so it would be better not to use the cookery saucepans! It may be possible to soak the material in the bath, if the school has one, or in a plastic washing-up bowl – in which case every child should be able to tie and dye his fabric at the same time.

Many different designs and patterns can be made if various items are tied up in the fabric before it is dyed.

Things to tie up

coin	yoghurt pot with stem (tied in
wax crayon	two places)
cotton-reel	shell
pencil (tied at both ends)	button
metal bottle-top	buckle

A useful book for handicrafts is *Something to Make* by Felicia Law (Penguin).

7 Music

Almost every child in the ESNs school will enjoy some form of music, whether it's pop records, singing or percussion band, and it can therefore be one of the most rewarding subjects to teach. However, it is sometimes rather noisy, and care should be taken that when one class has its music session the whole school is not disturbed. There should be time allowed for quieter music sessions too, when the child is simply expected to listen and think about the sounds he hears, rather than make sounds of his own. Without a tape recorder the sounds can be limited; with a tape, the teacher's imagination can run free by pre-recording varied and interesting sounds for the child to listen to.

Before a child can create his own variety of sounds he has to learn about the quality of those sounds; he needs to be taught high, low, fast, slow, soft and loud, and with the help of a tape recorder the teacher can heighten this awareness in each child.

However, many musical activities can be accomplished without a tape recorder, and the child should be encouraged to make his own sounds. He should practise making different sounds with parts of his body or household objects. He should learn to use his voice in many ways and eventually learn to sing. However, it is no use expecting a choir during singing sessions – it is rare for a mentally handicapped child to sing in tune. It is more important that he learns a large number of songs to teach him to remember words and so increase his vocabulary. He should not be expected to be word perfect on every song, but will derive great pleasure from singing, especially if he is taught a variety of tunes which he could even start to sing at his own leisure.

Making music can also involve making his own instruments to create different sounds, percussion instruments being the easiest to make. Each child in the older classes could be encouraged to make his own instrument, or perhaps make one for a child who is less capable – like a Special Care child. Once he has made his instrument, he only has to learn to play it, and this can often be harder than at first appears. Even if it only requires banging or shaking, the child needs to be taught to keep in time with the basic tune. Repetition and persistence are needed on the teacher's part if she is to create a tuneful percussion band.

When a child is involved in music it generally becomes a social activity, and an essential way to help the mentally handicapped child develop a more normal social awareness is to play games with him. If he was a normal child at an ordinary school, he and his friends would chant rhymes and play skipping or ball games. A mentally handicapped child rarely has the opportunity to play on an equal level with a normal child, so his teacher needs to play musical games with him, in order to provide similar social experience. Many of these games teach early number, for example '1, 2, 3, 4, 5 – Once I caught a fish alive!', and others teach order and sequence, like 'The farmer's in his den'. This singing game tells a story, and every time the child plays the game the characters appear in the same particular sequence. For instance:

> The farmer's in his den,
> The farmer wants a wife,
> The wife wants a child,
> The child wants a nurse – and so on.

On the following pages are suggestions for the many activities involved in both listening to and making music.

Listening

Commonplace sounds (5–16 years)
(Just close eyes and listen – in class, countryside, park or town. Some sounds can be pre-recorded.)

traffic	railway station	cat miaowing
car	market traders	dog barking
taxi	fairground	baby crying
motor-bike	rag and bone	distant voices
lorry	man	footsteps
bicycle bell	fire-engine	rain
aeroplane	ambulance	hail
helicopter	pigeons flapping	thunder
train	other birds	wind
	animals in zoo	

Summer sounds

cutting hedge	(a) manually	cricket (insect)
	(b) electrically	cricket (game)
lawnmower	(a) manual	church bells
	(b) electrical	frog croaking
bees		seaside
rustling grass		seagulls
children playing		birds singing

Household sounds (7–16 years)
(Pre-record and play back as a guessing game – not all at the same time!)

door bell	rattling cutlery	running tap
door chime	stirring tea	snipping scissors
telephone bell	spinning coin	sewing machine
telephone dial	striking match	sawing wood
alarm clock	banging door	electric drill
ticking clock	creaking door	hammering nail
chiming clock	locking door	typing
whistling kettle	vacuum cleaner	spraying aerosol
frying sizzle	(switching off)	rattling paper

Vocal, radio and TV sounds (7–16 years)

whisper	football crowd	auctioneer
shout	(cheering/	church congregation
foreign accent	chanting)	choir
dialect	tennis crowd	unaccompanied
American accent	(gasping)	singing
laughter	applause	opera
chatter	radio commenta-	pop group
	tor – fast/slow	Stanley Unwin
	(cricket, foot-	talking
	ball, golf, tennis,	
	horse-racing)	

Any of the above sounds can be played back to the child at the wrong speed purely for his amusement.

Records
The teacher herself will have many favourite records she likes to play to her group; likewise each child will have his own favourites – probably 'pop' records. However, a single disc usually lasts for three

minutes and this length of time will probably demand too much concentration for the younger child, so it is more satisfactory to play short excerpts from records. Below are listed various types of music to listen to, in addition to 'pop' songs.

electronic music
TV tunes (guessing game)
bagpipes
barrel organ
shoe-platter, Austrian dancing
flamenco, Spanish dancing

'Combine Harvester' (The Wurzels)
'Sparky and the Magic Piano'
'Laughing Policeman' (Charles Penrose)
'Pennsylvania 65000' (Glenn Miller)
'The Dambusters' March' (Eric Coates)

Some classical music:

The Humming Chorus from *Madame Butterfly* by Puccini
The Spinning Chorus from *The Flying Dutchman* by Wagner
Ritual Fire Dance from *El Amor Brujo* by Manuel de Falla
Flight of the Bumble-bee by Rimsky-Korsakov
Festival Overture 1812 by Tchaikovsky
Boléro by Ravel
Can-can music from *Orpheus in the Underworld* by Offenbach
Peter and the Wolf (story and music) by Prokofiev

Making sounds (all ages)
Even if the child is incapable of making these sounds himself, he will enjoy listening and watching the sounds made by his teacher. Many of these sounds could be used to teach a new tune or used as a different way to sing a favourite song. It can also be interesting to tape-record these sounds to play back later as a guessing game.

Making sounds with the mouth

ooo (push out lips)	brr	wind (nearly whistle)
ah (wide open mouth)	humm	
	brrm (fingers and lips)	clicking tongue
oh		growling
eeh (show teeth)	pop (smacking lips)	clicking teeth
loo (not lew)		gargling

Making sounds with the body

clapping hands	knocking knees	clicking fingers
slapping legs, etc.	knocking	tapping table
stamping feet	knuckles	scratching surface
tapping toes	drumming fingers	

Making sounds with household objects

wooden spoons to knock

metal spoons
bowls – assorted sizes
tins – assorted sizes   } to tap
pot-plant pots suspended
bottles containing varied
    levels of water

bunch of keys
clothes pegs
paper   } to rattle
small hard plastic
    food bag

strong elastic tightly attached
    to wall for pinging
small hard plastic food bag
marble rolling down slope
cardboard tube
whistle
clean rubber tube   } to blow
comb and tissue paper

Making sounds with instruments

whistle	small electric	drum
penny whistle	organ	maracas
recorder	chime bar	castanets
melodica	cymbal	shaker
glockenspiel	triangle	clapper
guitar	indian bells	banjo
piano	tambourine	

Instruments to make

Plastic shaker

Choose assorted shapes of plastic bottles e.g. empty washing-up liquid, fabric softener or baby lotion containers. Fill with any of the following:

sand	rice
salt	lentils
barley	seeds or bird-seed

Spread strong glue inside the screw top and replace – or block the open end of the container with a piece of dowelling or thick pencil, to provide the handle. Cover the outside with *Contact, Fablon* or any brightly-coloured material.

Metal shaker

Choose two tins the same size, with the lids completely removed and *no* jagged edges. Fill with any of the substances previously mentioned. Join the tins firmly together with sticky-tape or insulating tape. Cover the outside with *Contact, Fablon* or bright material.

Sound shaker (so named because it *sounds* like a shaker)

Glue sandpaper around two sticks; rub together.

Rattle can

Choose plastic or metal containers: fill with any of the following and then finish as for plastic or metal shakers:

dried peas or beans	nails
gravel	screws
pebbles	nuts or bolts

Tin-can rattle

Place 1 butter bean or 1 cotton-reel inside two tins. Finish as for metal shaker.

Bones

Wash, clean and dry neck bones from lamb chops. Thread them onto wire loop.

Bottle-tops

Nail coloured metal bottle-tops loosely onto a smooth block of wood, so that the tops rattle when the wood is shaken. Paint and decorate the wood.

Clappers

Choose two date-box lids and two wooden cotton-reels. Nail or glue a cotton-reel into the centre of each lid to make two clappers with handles. Paint and decorate upper part of lids (see diagram).

Football clapper

For this instrument three pieces of wood are needed: one larger, oblong piece and two square pieces preferably the same size. Drill

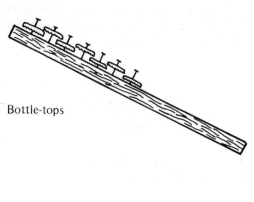

Bottle-tops

Clappers

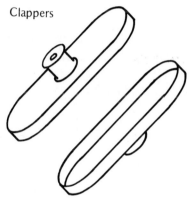

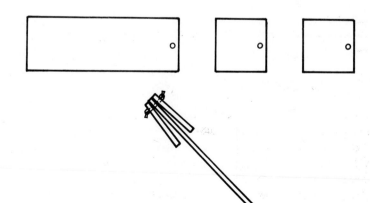

holes through all pieces in the centre $\frac{1}{2}$" from end. Thread strong cord or string through the holes and tie securely at either side, leaving some slack in the string for clapping (see diagram).

Coconut clappers
Possibly one of the oldest home-made clappers. Slice coconut in half — eat the flesh, drink the milk and dry the shell thoroughly. Clap shells together or on surface to sound like horses' hooves.

Walnut clappers
Tiny version of coconut clappers. Carefully remove nut from shell of walnut, clap two halves together very gently; or drill tiny hole at one end of each half and string together to play like castanets.

Single drum
Stretch old hot-water-bottle or heavy-duty polythene over large hollow tin (liver tins from the butcher, or catering-sized food tins are suitable). Fasten tightly with string using a slip knot. Cover with brightly coloured *Contact*, *Fablon* or material.

Bongo drums
Lash together two large plastic tubs, e.g. mincemeat tubs, with sticky tape. Leave the lids on and cover completely with *Contact*, *Fablon* or material.

Shake-a-bell
Sew bells onto knitted or crocheted bracelets. Place bracelet on Special Care child's wrist.

Tambourine
Join two paper plates together. Sew bells around the rim. Paint and decorate.

Making sounds in a band (7–16 years)
Basic rules for a simple band:
1　Introduce simple tunes which have 2 or 4 time.
2　Learn the beat first.
3　Teach the whole group on same instrument initially.
4　Orchestrate favourite songs and nursery rhymes.
5　Teach slow and fast.
6　The child must learn to listen musically and wait his turn.
7　Learn patterns of sound, e.g. boom-ta-ta, boom-ta-ta, diddly-dee, diddly-dee.

Suggested simple tunes to orchestrate:

Ding, dong, bell
Polly, put the kettle on
Bye, baby bunting
Ring-a-ring o' roses
Yellow submarine
If you're happy and you know it – Bang your drum (Shake a shaker, Blow your whistle)
Seventy-six trombones

Many other titles are listed under *Suitable songs* below.

Orchestrated singing (7–16 years)
Ideas for simple accompaniment:

1 One child plays tambourine to rhythm while teacher/class sing.
2 One child plays drum, another plays tambourine to rhythm while teacher/class sing.
3 Alternative instruments to be used as above: maracas, drum, shaker, clapper, rattle, bells.
4 Teacher to provide rhythm while class sings.
5 Whole class on same kind of instrument accompany teacher singing.
6 Tape-record class, school, radio or TV singing session and orchestrate.

Singing (all ages)
Teach new songs by:

1 humming tune
2 clapping rhythm
3 singing La La
4 saying words
5 singing words
6 child hums tune teacher sings words
7 play tune, on piano, recorder, guitar etc.
8 tape-record tune if necessary
9 teach several new songs regularly
10 try singing in rounds!

List of suitable songs
Nursery rhymes (3–7 years):

Humpty Dumpty
Jack and Jill
Goosey, goosey gander
Hickory, dickory, dock
Baa, baa, black sheep
Hush-a-bye, baby
Pussycat, pussycat, where have you been?
I had a little nut tree
Twinkle, twinkle, little star
Where has my little dog gone?
Little Miss Muffet
Lavender's blue, dilly, dilly
Frère Jacques
Ring-a-ring o' roses
See-saw, Margery Daw
Mary, Mary, quite contrary
Ding, dong, bell
Little Jack Horner
Little Bo-peep
Girls and boys come out to play
Bobby Shafto
Lucy Locket

Tom, Tom, the piper's son
Polly, put the kettle on
Sing a song of sixpence
Old King Cole
London Bridge is falling down
Oranges and lemons
Ride a cock-horse to Banbury Cross
Three blind mice
O, the grand old Duke of York
Hot cross buns
Hey diddle diddle
Pat-a-cake, pat-a-cake, baker's man
O dear, what can the matter be?
Bye, baby bunting
Here we go round the mulberry bush
Here we go gathering nuts in May

Favourite songs (7–16 years):

Kumbaya
Morningtown ride
Doh ray mi
Puff the magic dragon
Here we go Looby Loo
Old Macdonald had a farm
She'll be coming round the mountain
Michael Finnigan
There's a tiny house, by a tiny stream
My grandfather's clock
Wombling song

The red red robin
Zip-a-dee-do-dah! Zip-a-dee-ay!
Oh, when the saints
Qué sera, sera
Blowin' in the wind
Polly-wolly-doodle
What shall we do with the drunken sailor?
Strawberry fair
Save all your kisses for me
Where have all the flowers gone?
Oh me darlin' Clementine

We're all going to the zoo
tomorrow
Chick, chick, chick, chick,
chicken
I once had a meat ball
Rowntrees tots, please yourself
Nelly the elephant
Daddy wouldn't buy me a
bow-wow
Frog went a courtin'
A mouse lived in a windmill
in old Amsterdam
She wears red feathers
Oh, Suzannah
Lily the pink
I know an old lady who
swallowed a fly
Mud, mud, glorious mud
Tea for two
It's a long way to Tipperary
Oh, Mr Porter
Oh, soldier, soldier, will you
marry me?
Cockles and mussels (In
Dublin's fair city)

My eyes are dim, I cannot see
Daisy, Daisy, give me your
answer do
Li'l Liza Jane
Widdecomb Fair
Dashing away (with the
smoothing iron)
I'm Henry the Eighth, I am, I
am
There's a hole in my bucket,
dear Liza
Raindrops (keep falling on my
head)
Yellow submarine
I'd like to teach the world to
sing
I can sing a rainbow
Grandad
Where's your mama gone?
I can do anything better than
you!
Dance to thy Daddy, my little
laddie

Finger games and action rhymes (age according to suitability):

I can clap with my two hands
Incy, wincy, spider
Peter Pointer
Peter plays with one hammer,
this fine day
One finger one thumb, keep
moving
If you're happy and you know
it, clap your hands
Two little dicky birds sitting
on a wall
Miss Polly had a dolly who
was sick, sick, sick
Wind the bobbin up

I'm a little teapot, short and
stout
I hear thunder
Tall shops in the town
The wheels on the bus go
round and round
This little rabbit said, 'Let's
play'
An elephant goes like this and
that
Puffer train, puffer train
Row-row-row your boat
Heads and shoulders, knees
and toes

In a cottage in a wood
We are the red men, tall and
	straight
Five little ducks went
	swimming one day
Clap hands, Daddy comes
Five little speckled frogs, sat
	on a speckled log

John Brown had a little Indian
Tommy thumb, where are
	you?
Little Arabella Miller
Mr Hall is very tall (Mr Lynn
	is very thin)
Hands, knees and bumpsy-
	daisy

Christmas songs and carols:

God rest ye, merry gentlemen
Good King Wenceslas
Once in Royal David's city
The first Noël
Hark the herald angels sing
Ding, dong, merrily on high
O come, all ye faithful
Silent night

Away in a manger
We three kings
Twelve days of Christmas
Rudolf the red-nosed reindeer
We wish you a merry
	Christmas
Jingle bells

Hymns:

This little light of mine
Jesus bids us shine
Jesus loves me
Jesus, friend of little children
All things bright and beautiful
Morning has broken
Day is done

We plough the fields and
	scatter
Farmer, farmer, sow your seed
Down the air (God is sending
	rain)
Praise Him, praise Him

Musical games to play
In small groups:

Ring-a-ring o' roses
I'm a little sandy boy
London Bridge is falling
	down
Five currant buns in the
	baker's shop
The big ship sails down the
	alley-alley-o

Cobbler, cobbler, mend my
	shoe
Wind the bobbin up
The farmer's in his den
Here we go round the
	mulberry bush
Old Roger is dead
Poor Jenny sits a-weeping
Oranges and lemons

In large groups:
    Okey Cokey   Conga   Pass the parcel

Instructional games
At first the teacher will probably find it better to tell the class what to do after the music has stopped, as few children will retain the instruction through the music.

1   'When the music stops – do this'

curl up small	stand on one leg
stand very still	stand on tiptoes
tall as a tree	lie down
twisted and bent	hide
point to own name	sit down

2   'Do as I do' (change instruction during music)

trot like a horse	tip toe
walk like an elephant	stand up – sit down
slither like a snake	jump
clap hands	hop
stamp feet	skip
run on the spot	float like a balloon

3   'Bring me' or 'Show me'
This game makes the child look around his environment and teaches him to learn about the things around him. When the music stops 'Bring me' or 'Show me' something:

heavy	long
light	short
yellow (other colours)	smallest (e.g. shell)
pretty	largest (e.g. pine-cone)
round	plastic
very small	metal
hollow	wood
hard	bright
soft	dark

This can be extended to include numbers: 2 shells; 3 shakers; 1 *small* whistle/1 *large*.

Circle games
1   Chalk circles all over the floor: when music stops, get in a circle.
2   Make the circles coloured: when music stops, get in blue circle, etc.

3 Number the circles: when music stops, get in circle number 2, etc.

Elimination games

musical bumps
musical statues
musical chairs
who's wearing red?
who's not in the ring? (rings chalked over floor)
who's in the river? (parallel lines chalked on floor)

who's not on paper? (torn-up newspaper on floor)
who's wearing tights?
who's wearing pumps?
who's wearing tee-shirts? etc.
who's holding balloon? (pass balloon round)

Useful books

Apusskido — Songs for Children chosen by Beatrice Harrop (A. & C. Black)

Make Your Own Musical Instruments by M. Mandell and R. Wood (Bailey Bros)

Musical Activities with Young Children by Jean Gilbert (Ward Lock Educational)

This Little Puffin compiled by Elizabeth Matterson (Penguin)

Part 3

Physical Activities

8 Music and movement

Through music and movement the ESNs child can learn, with the teacher's guidance, to interpret music in the form of dance. During the music sessions the child has become used to hearing different kinds of music, possibly even moved to it; now he should be given the opportunity of movement in a large space. The difference here is that the movement should be disciplined. He should be encouraged to remember that a certain sequence of movements belongs to a particular piece of music. The movements can be instinctive or impulsive, initiated by the child or the teacher, but one of the aims behind music and movement is to develop the child's dance creativity. The child should first be encouraged to sit down quietly and listen to the music; later he can move to it intuitively and finally the teacher can give him suggestions and guidance.

The right choice of music is vital to the success of the lesson. It is important that it includes a great deal of contrast – loud and soft, fast and slow, for example. Any kind of music is suitable, classical, jazz and 'pop'. However, the teacher will interpret it better if she uses the music she knows and enjoys. Once again, the tape recorder will prove to be invaluable. It is so much easier for the teacher to use part of one tune, parts of several tunes joined together, or even stop and start the music at regular intervals with a tape recorder. In the first instance, she should select very simple music, such as a marching tune, and create one or possibly two basic movements for the child to make to that tune. As the child matures his interest should increase and the teacher will be able to introduce more complicated music and movements.

The mentally handicapped child has a good deal of physical energy, and music and movement is an interesting way for him to gain exercise and release some of that energy. It should also teach him to control and develop little-used muscles so that he will become more adept during the use of equipment in the gym. One of the major difficulties to overcome is to encourage each child to develop his own interpretation of the music. Often the mentally handicapped child's instinct is to copy, so that a situation develops whereby every child is moving in exactly the same direction at the same time. While this may be quite effective for a formal display, each child should also be encouraged to move independently to the music, interpreting it in his own way, with a little guidance from the teacher.

More difficulties arise as the child grows older, and heavier. When a child reaches ten stone, he looks a little incongruous flitting around like a butterfly to music from *Swan Lake*! His teacher, therefore, needs to create a dramatic situation, as opposed to music and movement, and incorporate adventure stories of land, sea and air into the lesson.

When planning a lesson, the teacher should be aware of three basic ways of travelling: first Motion, then Direction and finally Quality. For instance, once a child has learnt to jump (Motion), he should next discover *where* to jump (Direction) and then *how* to jump (Quality). When the child has discovered, with the teacher's help, the many different ways to jump, he could experiment with jumping to music, and maybe a story could evolve incorporating the music and movements. Later, he could use other ways of travelling and eventually a dance may evolve, created with an accumulation of skilled movements which the child has learnt over a series of music and movement lessons.

Whenever possible, the teacher should take part in the lesson – particularly if the group is following a radio broadcast (many of which are excellent for the younger child). She should dance and move with the group, giving praise, encouragement and help when required. The child who needs extra help may be physically handicapped in some way, or may be a rather introverted character. It is up to the teacher to encourage this child to relax so that he is able to move more freely.

On the following pages are useful words and ideas for movement and a list of music which should also be of value.

Motion

Free travelling

walking	flying	skipping
strolling	gliding	hopping
striding	scampering	jumping
swerving	sprinting	marching
twisting	scuttling	stepping
running	scurrying	tripping

galloping	crawling	shuffling
trotting	stamping	sauntering

Whole body

stretching	shaking	twitching
squirming	trembling	waving
wriggling	rocking	writhing
vibrating	rolling	teetering
shivering	swaying	tottering

Parts of body

wiggling fingers, toes	rolling head, shoulders
nodding head	circling arms, legs
shrugging shoulders	shaking all body parts
bending knees, body, arms	stretching all body parts
twisting body, arms	shrinking all body parts

Direction

Forwards

dashing	shooting	spurting
darting	wriggling	tiptoeing
creeping		

Backwards

sliding	wriggling	tiptoeing
creeping	shuffling	

Sideways

leaning	shuffling	tossing
rocking	stretching	flinging
swerving	striding	tilting

Up

shooting	erupting	springing up
launching	growing	rising up
exploding	stretching	

Down

collapsing	plunging	diving
tumbling	sinking	plummeting
subsiding	cascading	swooping
flopping		

Along
stretching	prowling	gliding
hovering	stalking	striding

Turning
twisting	twirling	corkscrew
swirling	spinning	swivel
whirling	wheeling	zig-zag
reeling	pivoting	circling
swerving	veering	

Quality

Heavy
trudging	hobbling	shambling
plodding	limping	slouching
dragging	shuffling	carrying
grovelling	lolloping	

Light
flying	tiptoeing	meandering
gliding	scurrying	wavering
hovering	skipping	prancing
swirling	dancing	airily
flitting	fluttering	gently
tripping	drifting	friskily

Fast
bursting	dashing	shooting
whizzing	speeding	darting
banging	whirling	

Slow
lingering	loitering	trudging
ambling	dragging	creeping
sauntering	crawling	

Continuous
inching	wandering	circling
meandering	swarming	slithering

Intermittent

flickering	looming	colliding
glimmering	fading	glittering
twinkling	lightning	jumping

Examples of movement

Heavy, slow or gradual

elephant	cat	giant
dinosaur	tortoise	Red Indian
lion	snail	burglar
old person	worm	monster
sad person	slug	King-Kong
person carrying heavy object		

Light, fast or sudden

swan	horse	bullet
bee	mouse	rocket
deer	arrow	fairy
spider	cannon-ball	snowflake
Jack-in-a-box	bubble	monkey
young baby	kangaroo	fireworks
happy person	bird	rain
balloon	paper	kite

Movement with a partner

pushing him away
rolling him around
dragging him around
chasing him
copying him, i.e. one is a mirror
working in total unison

Suggestions for types of dancing

busy dance
quiet dance
crooked dance
jumping dance
twisty dance
spiky dance
jerky dance
up-and-down dance (e.g. fireworks, umbrella)
strong dance
weak, floppy dance
repetitive dance (e.g. machine)
stop-and-go dance

Suggestions for imaginative topics

Animals
circus
jungle
underwater life
ugly duckling
strange creatures from another
planet

animals which jump (e.g.
kangaroo, rabbit, frog,
lamb)
animals which fly (e.g. bat,
bird, insect)
frightening animals
friendly animals

People

magician	giant	Dalek
clown	fairy	astronaut
witch	robot	tightrope walker
at the fairground		

Toys

| jack-in-a-box | rag doll | train set |
| wooden puppet | ball | teddy bear |

Machinery

| clocks | factory | wheels |
| cars | television | |

Dramatic, adventure
fairies and giants
fairies and witches
cats and mice
cops and robbers
cowboys and Indians
warlords and Daleks
any TV hero currently popular

arrival on new planet
hypnotist and victim
snake and charmer
ghosts
pirates
escape
Alice in Wonderland
stormy weather

Suitable music

Classical music
In addition to the list on page 94, the following music is suggested:
Young Person's Guide to the Orchestra by Britten
Peer Gynt Suite by Grieg
Swan Lake by Tchaikovsky

Night on the Bare Mountain by Mussorgsky
Pictures at an Exhibition by Mussorgsky
Polovtsian Dances from *Prince Igor* by Borodin
The Overture from *William Tell* by Rossini
Slavonic Dances by Dvořák
Carnival of the Animals by Saint-Saëns
Air on the G String by Bach
The Sorcerer's Apprentice by Dukas
The Planets Suite by Holst
Fingal's Cave Overture by Mendelssohn

Popular music
music from James Bond films
theme from *Exodus*
Zorba's Dance
Dambusters' March
The Entertainer (Scott Joplin)
Puppet on a String
Hava Nagila

Hernando's Hideaway
Take the 'A' Train
Spanish Flea
Popcorn
Una Paloma Blanca
Electronic Music
A Walk in the Black Forest

Music from shows:
An American in Paris
West Side Story
Cabaret
Paint Your Wagon
Hair

Fiddler on the Roof
Jesus Christ Superstar
Joseph and the Amazing
    Technicolour Dreamcoat

Many long-playing records are available with selected instrumental music played by large bands or orchestras, and some of these are often suitable for music and movement themes. Another useful record is *Listen, Move and Dance*, Nos. 1–3 (HMV).

The following books will be helpful to the teacher interested in music and movement for young children:

Creative Dance in the Primary School by Joan Russell (Macdonald & Evans)
Listen and Move Series, Nos. 1 and 2 (Macdonald & Evans)
Musical Activities with Young Children by Jean Gilbert (Ward Lock Educational)

9   Physical education

Nowadays most ESNs schools include PE on their timetables. At one time it was thought too dangerous or unsuitable for a mentally handicapped child to climb wall bars, swing from a trapeze or even jump on a trampoline. Modern thinking is to encourage as much physical activity as possible, developing climbing and balancing skills which even a normal child may not achieve.

Many modern ESNs schools are lucky enough to be built with gymnasium equipment in the main hall. Some equipment needs to be put away after use; others, like the trestles or wall bars, are permanently out and the child is taught when he is allowed on the equipment and when he should not be on it.

The capabilities of each child vary considerably. An active mongol, for example, may enjoy climbing on everything and reach the top of the trestles or ropes in a very short time. Yet there is a big difference between him and the partially sighted or physically handicapped child who trembles at the thought of walking along a form! Generally, though, it can be said that if a child has enough confidence to climb high, he is unlikely to fall, unless he loses his concentration. Unfortunately there are some exceptions in the ESNs school. Perhaps a child with severe epilepsy wishes to climb high up. Should his teacher allow him to explore high places and cover the floor with mats to cushion a possible fall? Or should she keep him on a lower level for safety's sake, but deprive him of exploring the high places he wants to discover? The teacher is in a dilemma and it is her responsibility; she must take into account the physical size of the child, his general activities, the effects of his medication and the wishes of his parents – but the final decision is hers.

However, PE involves not only the use of large apparatus. It includes physical gymnastics, bending, stretching, rolling, forward and backward movements as well as the use of small apparatus like balls, beanbags, hoops and skipping ropes. The teacher must provide varied and interesting PE sessions. She could even create a dramatic situation on apparently simple apparatus. For instance, three forms could be set out to make a triangle and the class encouraged to walk along the forms, being careful not to fall into the 'water', which is represented by the area inside the triangles. This is a very simple PE 'game' and almost every child will enjoy balancing, even if one or two need to hold the teacher's hand. If it becomes too easy, one of the forms could be turned over so that more skill is needed to balance on the narrower bar.

Changing for the PE session also gives the child an excellent opportunity to practise undressing and dressing himself, and can sometimes give the teacher her only chance to observe how capable each child is and how much more teaching he needs in that respect. The younger classes will obviously need much more help than the older child, but it is a very important part of the routine that he should be taught to put on his own jumper, shoes and socks, as well as take them off.

When setting out larger equipment such as trestles, boxes, the trampoline and so on, the teacher has to provide an apparently spacious gym, so that each child has sufficient room to move about from one piece of equipment to another. This is particularly noticeable if the gym is also the main hall, which other people need to walk through or around during a PE session. It can be quite embarrassing when visitors have to duck under bridges, dodge ropes and be careful not to trip over mats on their 'obstacle course' round the school! A path should always be left clear and the hall should look like a well-planned, interesting environment.

Wherever possible each child should be encouraged to help set out and put away the equipment – this is often as important as the lesson itself. The forms could be put away quickly, with one child at either end, although the teacher herself will have to help and guide the larger equipment into position. With the smaller equipment, each child could take turns in collecting it and this could involve the use of numbers. For instance: Teacher – 'There were twelve hoops – how many have you got?' Child – 'Three'. The child is then encouraged to collect the rest of the hoops, counting as he goes along.

On the following pages are lists of activities and uses of equipment for the PE sessions in school.

Physical skills

These should be regarded as basic limbering-up activities and, while the younger child may only be able to run or possibly jump for two or three minutes without getting out of hand, the older child should be able to accomplish many of the following skills with relative ease. However, the teacher of the older teenager should be conscious of the child's age and probable size, and not make him seem incongruous by giving him skills like 'bunny' jumps to practise.

Moving (5–13 years)
    running in all directions (i.e. not all round and round the room in one way)
    running fast
    running noisily
    running on tiptoe
    running on the spot
    running with occasional jumps – high, low
    jumping on the spot (feet together)
    jumping in a pattern (feet apart, together, apart)
    turn and jump
    clapping while jumping – high, low
    'bunny' jumps (crouched down)
    hop on one foot – other foot
    hop on the spot
    slow hops, quick hops
    skipping (hopping quickly from one foot to another)

Lying down (7–13 years)
Find a 'space' (conception of space is very important).
1   *lie on back:*
    stretch legs and arms wide (try to touch neighbour)
    roll over onto tummy, back again
    curl up, bend arms and legs
    legs in air, cycling motion
    legs wide apart in air, one leg down, one up
    bring legs together towards head, try to touch floor behind head
    legs down, trunk up
    try to touch knees with nose
    rock trunk from side to side, keep legs straight
    swing leg across to opposite arm; swing other leg
    try to touch toes, keep legs straight
2   *lie on tummy:*
    stretch legs and arms wide (try to touch neighbour)
    push up with hands, bring head, shoulders, chest up from floor
    bring legs up too

try to grasp legs with hands while rocking tummy on floor
relax, pretend to sleep

Standing up (7–16 years)
Find a space:
    stretch legs, arms wide apart, swing around, try to touch neighbour
    stretch fingers, toes; wiggle them
    stretch arms, hands, fingers high in air
    up on tiptoe, stretch legs too
    drop arms down suddenly, touch toes
    swing arms up and down
    swing arms from side to side, twist shoulders, chest, hips, trunk
    floppy like a rag doll, bend knees; arms, shoulders sag
    shake and shiver all over, hands, arms, shoulders, head, body, legs
    shake one foot, then other foot
    start to shake in one place (e.g. finger), extend to hand, arm, body,
        etc.
    stand still
    kick one leg high in the air, then other leg
    bend one knee up to chin, then other knee
    crouch down suddenly
    jump up quickly
    slowly lower self down
    very slowly rise up, without using hands
    bend over sideways, other side
    twist, shake all over, then stand still

Small equipment
The use of small equipment helps the child develop fine control of his
muscles and improves his hand/eye coordination. The younger child
will only be able to concentrate for a short period on any one piece of
apparatus. As he becomes older he will develop skills until eventually
he is very adept and may even be able to play complex activities such
as 'two balls'.

Small ball (all ages)
Airflow balls (plastic balls with air holes) are the most serviceable and
they are safe to use indoors, the only disadvantage being that they are
difficult to bounce.

    Activities
    roll ball along floor

roll ball down tilted form
roll ball along arm
pass ball from one hand to the other
pass ball behind back
pass ball under leg, changing hands
throw ball high in air, catch it
throw ball at wall, catch it, two hands, one hand
kick ball, with each foot in turn
aim ball at skittles
play 'two ball' – juggle two balls in air or at wall

With partner:
throw ball to partner, catch it
hands and ball behind back, partner guesses which hand has ball
roll ball between partner's legs
roll ball under partner's 'bridge', made by him being on 'all fours'
partner tries to hit ball with bat, e.g. padder bat
partner tries to hit ball with hand

In groups or teams:
roll ball between several legs
roll ball through partner's legs at a distance – competition
pass ball over heads (all in a line) – man at back becomes front man

Bean bag (all ages)
Many activities with a bean bag are similar to those played with a ball.
There are some differences, however, which the child is expected to
discover. Bean bags are very easy to make: fill a square, cloth bag
two-thirds full of dried beans or peas and seal the bag. Remember not
to wash them or the beans will swell!

Activities
slide bean bag across floor – how far does it slide?
slide bean bag down tilted form
drop bean bag on floor, listen to sound
throw bean bag high in air, catch it, two hands, one hand
throw bean bag at wall – what happens?
balance bean bag on head, elbow, hand, foot, knee, shoulder, back,
    etc.
pass bean bag from hand to hand
toss bean bag from hand to hand
aim bean bag at skittles

put bean bag on floor, draw circle round it with toe, heel, other foot
jump over bean bag
hop over bean bag
walk with bean bag between knees
kneel down, push bean bag with nose, hands behind back
lie down, place bean bag between feet, throw it in the air, catch it

With partner:
throw bean bag over partner's head
slide bean bag through partner's legs
slide bean bag under partner's bridge
partner guesses which hand holds bean bag behind back
throw bean bag to partner, catch it with two hands, one hand
walk with partner holding bean bag together not using hands, e.g.
    with shoulders, forehead and chin, elbows, etc.

Hoop (all ages)

Three sizes usually available — 18", 24" and 30" diameter, made in plastic, bamboo or wood. The plastic hoops usually break easily at the join, the wooden hoops tend to splinter, so the bamboo hoop, although it is the most expensive, is the most durable. However, even this type should not be expected to last indefinitely.

Activities
place hoop on floor
step into hoop
pull hoop up over body, hold high above head
drop hoop down — listen to clatter
jump in and out of hoop
hop in and out of hoop
run in and out of hoop
jump all around hoop
hop all around hoop
run all around hoop
walk all around the edge of hoop
pretend hoop is steering wheel — 'drive' car, avoiding accidents
place all hoops on floor — run in-between, avoiding 'puddles'
spin hoop, jump into it before it stops
apply backspin, making it return
roll hoop across floor
'lasso' skittle with hoop
spin hoop around arm, leg, waist (as in hula-hoop)

With partner:
partner holds hoop – jump through, climb through, stride through, slither through, without touching hoop
walk together, both inside hoop
run around room both holding hoop, two hands, one hand

Large ball (all ages)
The plastic football type is very serviceable, but the teacher must be conscious of the possibility of accidents and should control all uses of the large ball indoors. The beach ball, inflatable type, is popular, but the child may have difficulty manoeuvring such a lightweight ball.

Activities
holding ball between hands, sit down or kneel down
place ball between feet, throw it in the air
walk with ball between feet, knees
bounce the ball
pat-bounce the ball, count the bounces
run and bounce the ball
spin the ball
walk with ball balanced on hand
bounce the ball all around self
roll the ball and chase it
kick the ball, chase it, kick it with other foot
dribble the ball around the room, very slowly
lie down, holding ball between feet, and move legs up, sideways, down
aim ball at skittles
bounce ball over objects, e.g. skittles, cane
push ball with one hand

With partner:
kick ball to partner
throw ball to partner
bounce ball to partner
roll ball to partner
pass ball over head to partner
pass ball through legs to partner
roll ball under partner's 'bridge'
while moving, throw ball to partner

Skittles and canes (7–16 years)

These are very useful items in the small equipment list. The wooden skittles can be 12" or 24" high and have a groove in the top on which to rest the 3' canes. Choose stout canes and bind the ends with sticky-tape to prevent splitting.

Activities
provide series of jumps around the room
wriggle under 'jumps' on tummies and backs
jump over series of jumps low to high
series of low jumps very close together – two steps apart
lie canes on floor, walk along, jump over
place skittles in pairs, weave in and out, like a slalom
roll small ball in-between skittles
knock skittles over with ball
'lasso' skittle with hoop
kneel down, hold skittle in either hand, try to walk on 'all fours'

Additional useful small equipment
rope – long and short
wooden blocks – some with grooves, for lower jumps
badminton and squash racket
rounders, table-tennis and padder bat (similar to large table-tennis bat, made from plywood but with no rubber pads)
ping-pong ball
shuttlecock
rubber quoits
high jump (with cane and measuring stops)

Large equipment (all ages)

Even the child in the Special Care class should be given the opportunity to use the large apparatus. He will certainly benefit from the change in environment and may enjoy the large space in the gym or hall. A partially-sighted Special Care boy may thoroughly enjoy hanging upside-down from a trapeze, feeling the floor with his hands. He could control all his own movements and be able to get down when he wanted a change. Every child in the school should be encouraged to explore various forms of large equipment.

Trestles and towers

Trestles are usually strong aluminium frames, some of which fold away, while some are provided with ladders and parallel bars. Towers are square-shaped wooden frames of varying heights and usually accompanied by slides and ladders. These two types are basic climbing frames which the teacher has to build up. They can be linked in any of the following ways (*all* with an abundance of safety mats):

high up
low down
with high, steep slide
with low gradual slide
with form or ladder attached on a slant, low to high
with ladder placed high above form
together in a long line
together in a square

Slide
Sloping wooden form, sometimes part of climbing frame.

Activities
slide down on tummy, head first; feet first
slide down on back, feet first
slide down upright, legs together; legs astride
slide down upright, legs astride, backwards
pull up sloped form, on tummy
crawl up form on hands and knees
crawl up form using hands and feet
walk up form forwards; backwards
walk down form, forwards; backwards
crawl down form, forwards; backwards

Ladders and ladder bridges
Ladder bridges are usually made of wood and freestanding, having rungs along the top and up either side. Ladders can be metal or wood and are made to be attached to trestles or towers.

Activities
crawl over ladder bridge
crawl beneath ladder bridge (like a monkey)
swing under ladders – hand over hand
hang upside-down from knees
holding rungs under bridge, swing legs up, push them through rungs

Wooden forms

These essential pieces of apparatus are of a regular shape but can vary in size. They can be used flat on the floor or are provided with hooks to fasten on to other apparatus. Most schools have many forms to use as bridges, slides or merely for balancing.

Activities
balance – walk along; run along; walk along backwards; walk along, heel-to-toe; count number of big strides; tiptoe along
astride – forwards; backwards
slither along on tummy, forwards; backwards
slither along on back, forwards; backwards
jump over form
turn form over and balance along narrow beam
place three forms in a triangle, walk all around, without falling off
attach to small frame for low jump off
attach to trestles, to make bridges, slides and use as above

Trampoline

Several sizes are available, the sturdy, square-shaped type (approximately $4^{1}/_{2}$–5 sq. ft.) being most serviceable, while the tiny one with a handrail is useful for the younger child. Very large, gymnastic ones are rather cumbersome and unnecessary for the average ESNS school. A mentally handicapped child can become quite proficient at jumping on the sturdy, square trampoline.

Activities
jump up and down
clap hands while jumping
count jumps
jump in a pattern: legs apart, together, apart, together, apart
arms wide when legs apart, arms straight when legs together
jump up, kneel down, jump up, kneel
jump up, sit down, jump up, sit
count three jumps then sit
jump up, turn in air, land, jump
teacher uses whistle for child to stop
teacher holds red band for stop, green for go
two children hold hands, jump together

Rings

These consist of two wooden rings suspended on the end of ropes with an adjustable height. They have many uses for practising good control of muscles.

Activities
pull self off ground, holding rings, swing legs
swing freely with rings in armpits, holding rings
holding rings, swing legs up until parallel to the ground
holding rings, swing legs up into the air, until parallel to the ropes
holding rings, somersault through the air with careful backward movement

Trapeze
This is very similar to the rings and involves the control of muscles in the same way. It is a wooden bar suspended from two ropes of an adjustable height.

Activities
swing legs freely, holding bar with hands
hang head and torso over one side, legs over the other side of the bar, swing
hold bar tightly with hands, swing legs up to bar and down again
swing legs up to bar, push them through until hanging by hands and legs
let go of hands and remain swinging upside-down from backs of knees (child should be able to touch ground with hands)

Ropes
Usually four to eight ropes are suspended from runners in the ceiling. They can be knotted by the teacher at the base to provide a seat or help the child begin to climb the rope.

Activities
hold tightly on to rope and swing
sit on knot, hold tightly with hands, swing
use form to help child climb on to ropes
stand on knot and swing, holding tightly with hands
gripping the rope tightly between knees and crossed-over feet, climb the rope
climb up one rope, and down another, *not* sliding
swing on rope and jump off (imaginary game – Tarzan)
swing holding on to two ropes
run up to rope, jump on it, swing, jump off

Box and vaulting horse

These two pieces of high apparatus are used mainly for jumping from, along or over. They are both wooden with a padded top. The horse has adjustable legs and the box will split into several sections to vary its height. A springboard should be used in conjunction with either the box or the horse to help the child jump onto the apparatus.

Activities
run up to, climb on, jump off
jump from board, land astride, jump off
sit on box, slide off
low, half box − jump over; somersault along box top; slide across on tummy, backwards, forwards; slide across on back, backwards, forwards
stand on end − jump very high, off
turn when jumping off
clap hands in air when jumping off
somersault off the end
stand on end − jump with legs very wide

All the above jumps will be improved if the child is encouraged to finish his movements tidily, either by doing a somersault and standing up or simply by standing straight.

Additional useful large apparatus
scrambling net
wooden boxes
hidey hole
barrel
suspended tyre
tunnel
stools (soft top, metal supports)
parallel bars
beam
wall bars

10   Sports and games

Sports and games are natural activities to follow all the skills learnt in PE and it is up to the staff of the school to provide as much variety of skills and physical activities as possible. The ESNs child needs a good deal of exercise to keep him physically healthy, and sports and games should keep him energetic, although the more sluggish child may need much encouragement and persuasion before joining in.

The school could organize a Sports Day and invite parents and friends to come and enjoy every child's achievements. If it becomes an annual event, then guests will be able to see the progress that each child makes as he moves up the school. It is important on such an occasion to involve every child, even those with physical handicaps. For instance, a partially sighted child could take part in a three-legged race. There could be a shuffle-bottom race for those who cannot walk, and a Dress the Baby race involving the severely handicapped Special Care child; maybe even the staff could have a race! What is important is to involve the whole school. It would be an added attraction and incentive if the winner of each race was presented with a certificate as a reminder to him and his parents of his achievement.

There are, however, other kinds of sports which are not connected with a sports day event. It is vital, for instance, that the capable mentally handicapped child should learn to swim, and therefore the school should organize weekly trips to the swimming baths, if possible with a qualified swimming instructor to teach him. He should be encouraged to respect but not fear water, and, while he is learning he could wear inflatable armbands or 'swimsafe' vests. He should be given a certificate when he has swum a length, like other children, and be encouraged to go swimming at weekends and holidays with his parents.

As many sports and games are social activities, it is usually the older ESNs child who will learn to play games by following rules. A younger child, say below seven years, will probably be too introverted to play organized games in a group. He will be limited to very simple chanting games and rhymes, rather than the more complicated sporting games. It is important that the older child learns to be guided by even the simplest rules and accepts that they are necessary for the games to be successful.

Football is a popular team game and, like many other team games, it could be simplified and played in ESNs schools. The teacher could install goalkeepers and encourage every other member of the class to run after and kick the ball. Opposing teams could be defined by the use of coloured bands (if the class cannot discriminate colours clearly enough then one side could be without bands). Providing the rules are kept to a minimum and are very simple, the mentally handicapped child will derive a great deal of pleasure from a simple football game. The older class could perhaps even form a team and play against a similar group from another school or even the nearby Adult Training Centre, on a regular basis.

There are many other sports and games which the mentally handicapped child rarely has the opportunity of experiencing. Ordinary children play simple games in the street, such as Tag, or Hide and Seek, but the ESNs child does not often play in the street. If he did, the other children would probably not have enough patience to teach him their games. Therefore it is up to the teacher to provide opportunities for him to learn some children's games. Nearly every ESNs school has an outside play area which is often only used during the summer months, due to the fact that it takes such a long time for the few staff on duty at playtime to see that each child is properly clad against the cold weather. Hence the winter playtimes are sometimes restricted to indoor play. However, the teacher could take out her own class daily and teach the basic rules of many simple children's games.

Periodically there are fashions in children's games, such as yo-yos or hula hoops and the mentally handicapped child should have the opportunity to play with these items. With plenty of practice he could become proficient at using them and this may provide a liaison between him and an ordinary child. If he has the opportunity to play with normal children in the street, he would be able to play on a par with them, and they may learn that he is not such an oddity at all.

The following pages contain ideas for many different kinds of sports and games which the mentally handicapped child will enjoy and benefit from, socially, physically and intellectually.

Swimming (7–16 years)
Regular visits to local baths with qualified swimming instructor. Use

of inflatable armbands and other safety equipment for non-swimmers. Award certificates for achievement.

Follow-up activities: animals that swim, e.g. bears, fish, horses, dogs. Historical swimming costumes. Swimming and diving sports in Olympic Games.

Horse riding (7–13 years)
Provided purely for interest and experience. It is unlikely that he will ever ride alone. Helmets *must* be provided.

Follow-up activities: visit stables, feed horses, help rub down horses. Sport to do with horses – horse racing, polo, show jumping. *Black Beauty* – story of horse.

Ball games

Football (5–16 years)
Youngest child can play at kicking large ball, then learn to kick ball into net. Use coloured bands for teams. Team game – child learns to pass ball to another child. Form a school team and play regularly against similar group, e.g. Adult Training Centre.

Follow-up activities: Visit local football club grounds during day; attend local football match; make histogram of favourite teams – or four or five top teams – use team colours for blocks.

Variation: Instead of net, use skittles to be defended by three or four. When skittle is knocked down, defender changes places with attacker.

Rounders (7–16 years)
Easy rules – could be played more. Underarm bowl, ball is hit, player runs around four posts in a square. Similar rules to cricket, use small rubber or tennis ball and any bat. Proper rounders bat difficult to use.

Variation: Child stands at each of four posts, with bat. Ball is batted to each child in turn.

Cricket (7–16 years)
Another bat and ball game. Bowler tries to knock down wicket with ball. Batsman tries to hit ball. Use soft rubber or tennis ball.

Variation: French cricket. Batsman protects legs below knee. Bowler tries to hit batsman's lower legs. Batsman can turn. If leg is hit, batsman and bowler change places. There can be several bowlers.

Badminton (7–16 years)
Use shuttlecock instead of ball. Provide bat or racket for each child.

The aim is to keep the shuttle off the ground, hitting it back and forth across the net.

Variation: Teacher and class bat shuttle between each other, keeping it up.

Other ball games

1 Chalk or paint marks on wall for child to aim at (above or below) with ball, or bat and ball.
2 Knock down skittle with rolling ball.
3 Ball tag – Person who is 'on' throws ball to try and hit others below knees. Person hit becomes 'on'.
4 Roll ball between legs, skittles, etc.
5 Throw ball through vertical hoop.

Team ball games

1 Teams stand in lines:
  leader passes ball back over heads; passes ball back between legs; passes small ball back with one hand, down the side, child at back changes hands and ball is returned, one hand at a time to leader; bounce ball over team's heads; throw ball over team's heads; team lies down – roll ball over team.
2 Children stand in ring:
  large ball passed around hand to hand in front; small ball passed around behind children – child in middle guesses where ball is. (At intervals a different child *pretends* to be handling ball.) Child in centre bounces ball to child in ring; child in centre pats ball to child in ring; child in centre throws ball to child in ring, who throws/pats/bounces it back.

Street games (10–16 years)

Many of the street games involve a child being 'on' or 'it'. To make a child 'on', the group has a 'dip'. This involves counting with a chant, such as:

Dip, dip, dip
My blue ship
Sailing on the water
Like a cup and saucer
I say you are IT.
(To be chanted while counting feet, fists or children.)

or

One potato
Two potato

Three potato – four
Five potato
Six potato
Seven potato – more
I say you are IT.
(Last person pointed to becomes 'it' or 'on'.)

These are relatively simple chants for the older ESNs child to learn, and when the person to be 'on' has been decided, the following games can be played:

Tag or Tick

One child is 'on' and chases others; child who is touched then becomes 'on'. Variations:

1 Couple tick: two children are 'on' together, chase class while holding each other's hands – need to touch two others. (This is a good way to teach tick, as teacher and assistant could alternate being 'on' with a different child.)

2 Chain tick: one child is 'on' first, chases others; as each child is touched he joins the chain until all the class are holding hands.

3 Statue tick: one child is 'on' and as each child is touched, he must stand still, like a statue. Continue until every child is a statue, except one who is 'on'.

In many of the above games the teacher or her assistant could be 'on' at first to help the child understand the game.

Hide and Seek

Very similar to Tick but child who is 'on' closes his eyes whilst remainder hide. He must find them.

Variation: The ones who are found help to seek the others.

Touchstone or Footstone

Not unlike Hide and Seek but child who is 'on' stands near particular stone. Those in hiding must try to return and 'touch stone' without being seen.

Hop-scotch

This is rather complicated even for the most capable ESNs child, but it could be an interesting individual session for the teacher and child. The skills involved are: hopping; jumping, feet apart and together; counting; aiming small stone (or bean bag).

Fashionable games

yo–yo	jacks
hula–hoop	marbles
frisbee	skipping
pogostick	'two ball'
roller–skates (or skateboard)	

Sports Day races

The main aim of Sports Day is to encourage each child to run to the finishing line, and this can sometimes be difficult. It is a good idea to acquire some bunting from a petrol company and encourage each child to run to the flags. They are bright and colourful and will attract the child's attention. It is also important to be absolutely clear who the winners are, so a member of the staff who knows every child very well should be at the winning post making a note of the winners' names. Each race should be started with a whistle or similar sudden, sharp sound. Suggestions for races are given below, roughly listed in order of difficulty:

1 *Flat race* Run from start to finish, distance according to ability.
2 *Bean-bag race* Run to bean bag, pick it up, run back with it.
3 *Hoop race* Run to hoop, sit in it.
4 *Bag and hoop race* Run to bean bag, pick it up, run with it and place in hoop.
5 *Head-balancing race* Walk to finish with bean bag on head.
6 *Egg and spoon race* (Use a brick or bead and spoon.) Walk, carefully balancing bead on spoon, to finish.
7 *Relay race* Requires at least two teams. First child runs with stick, passes stick to second child who runs with stick to third child, etc. First team to finish wins.
8 *Shuffle-bottom race* For any child who is mobile but cannot walk – encourage any form of movement. Make distance short.
9 *Dress-the-baby race* Older child has young severely handicapped Special Care child for partner. Older child runs to pile of clothes and puts hat, scarf and blanket on 'baby'. 'Baby' wins.
10 *Balancing race* Wooden forms placed lengthways along course. Child must walk balancing along form, then run to finish.
11 *Sliding race* Wooden forms, as above, but child must slide along form on tummy, or back.
12 *Three-legged race* Two children run together while middle two legs are bound. Partner one capable child with less capable one.
13 *Hurdles* Place skittles and canes apart to make hurdles.

14 *Throw-a-bag*   Helpers needed to hold hoops vertically. Child throws bean bags through hoops; winner counts three.

15 *Sack race*   Place sacks halfway across course. Child runs to sack; once in it, jumps to finish.

16 *Wheelbarrow race*   For strong children. One child walks on hands whilst other holds him by the legs. (Usually a good deal of fun!)

17 *Blind man's three-legged race*   Two capable children are bound together, but one is blindfolded.

18 *Obstacle race*   Children race through a series of obstacles, e.g. jump over cane, scramble under blanket, climb through hoop, pick up bean bag, run to finish.

19 *Tug-of-war*   Teams required and *very* thick, strong rope. Each team pulls on rope until one team falls over.

20 *First-dressed race*   Place individual piles of clothes in front of each child to race, e.g. hat, shirt, skirt, large shoes, scarf. First child properly dressed wins.

21 *Best-dressed or funniest-dressed race*   Place large pile of assorted clothes (hats, shoes, shirts, skirts, scarves, cardigans, coats, etc.) in centre of course. Children rush to pile and child who is best dressed at end wins. (At least four articles of clothing should be worn.) The visitors could choose winner.

11   The Special Care child

The Special Care child has been included in this part of the book because nearly all the activities he can accomplish are physical activities. His teacher may need to physically move him from one situation to another, to give him bodily contact with another person, child or adult. She also has to see to all his physical needs, feed him, wash him, toilet and dress him.

The term 'Special Care' does not define a particular disability, but the child's needs. For example one child may be disruptive, hyperactive and need Special Care to restrain him and stop him from disrupting other classes; another may require Special Care if he is severely physically handicapped; and so many ESNs schools have a Special Care class or Unit where this type of child can be properly catered for.

As previously observed, much of the teaching involved in a Special Care class is physical work, and the teacher must become aware of the needs of each individual child. For example, if a child is used to lying down all day, because of his disability, he should be raised up, maybe in a standing frame, or even higher into a hammock, perhaps, so that he has a different aspect of the classroom. He could also be suspended in a secure harness (like a Baby Bouncer) and have his feet plunged into warm water, or sand to give him different experiences.

The methods used to induce a certain type of very stubborn child to move may, at first glance, seem to be rather harsh, but, as he needs incentive to move, different methods have to be used to encourage him to shuffle or stagger about the classroom. For instance he could be placed in awkward corners, on different apparatus, his drinks could be positioned just out of reach and he should have to encounter regular problems and obstacles which will, hopefully, motivate him into moving.

Surprisingly this child can be just as stubborn, awkward and determined as a normal child and, possibly because of his additional handicaps, he can be even more demanding; he must be taught the meaning of 'No', or at least to respond to the cross voice of the teacher. Nearly every child in the Special Care class can make his needs known. He will cry when uncomfortable, hungry or cross and chortle when he's content. It is the teacher's task to recognize these sounds and give the appropriate response. Much of the language of the Special Care child depends on his understanding, rather than his actual use of language. The teacher should therefore use as much language as possible with frequent gestures and spontaneous songs.

Useful words:

No!	Bye Bye!	Da Da
Come Here!	Hello!	Mum Mum
Sit Down!	Again!	Na Na
Stand Up!	More!	Classroom (pointing)
Thank You!	All gone!	Toilet (pointing)

The Special Care child is not, however, totally silent; he can make many noises, some will be unusual and it can be interesting to tape-record these sounds and play them back at a more quiet moment. Sometimes the child will not appear to notice, but he may just hesitate in his current activity and seem to listen.

Many of his needs will be the same as those for a baby – but they will last for years and it can become tedious to play baby games for many years. He is rarely taken out by his parents, who are probably embarrassed by him, and it is therefore a good idea to take him out of the classroom regularly. The Special Care child rarely has a change in his environment, but he needs it, possibly more than the more active ESNs child. Singing, too, is a great stimulus, and the teacher could sing spontaneously during the day or have a singing session with the class in a group and use a tape recorder for extra volume. Another class could be brought in to sing to the Special Care group, or play their instruments; records of all kinds (of choirs, orchestras, 'pop' music and nursery rhymes) should also be played – the main idea is constantly to stimulate the Special Care child and not treat him as being in a unit completely separate from the school.

On the following pages are some suggestions for teaching the Special Care child and some charts to record his ability.

Feeding

For a child in the Special Care class, to learn to feed himself is one of the highest peaks of his achievement, yet it can take him many years to accomplish. Almost any child, unless he is too severely physically handicapped, can learn to sit at a table and feed himself using a spoon and dish. Perseverance and patience are needed to achieve results. It is important, however, that the relationship between the teacher and child during dinner time should be a similar relationship to that between the mother and her baby whilst feeding. That is to say that the teacher (and her assistants) should concentrate on feeding one child at a time and not, as sometimes happens, sit the class all in a row and push food into one open mouth after another. The food should be placed where he can see it and enough time taken over feeding to maintain a calm environment.

A certain type of child may have difficulty in making the correct oral movements for eating and the teacher should encourage him to chew and swallow correctly. The spoon should be placed near the back of the mouth, flat on the tongue, and the child should be taught to work the food away from the spoon himself. This means that the spoon should not be drawn through his lips or teeth in order to clean the spoon, but the child should be encouraged to suck the food away using his own muscles.

Toileting and dressing

It is very tempting to hurry through toileting and dressing when the child arrives each morning, in order to have more time to teach him. However, it is a vital part of the day for the Special Care child. He needs extra help and prolonged teaching in this respect because it may possibly be years before he grasps the idea of toileting fully. He should be well praised at appropriate opportunities and a good routine should be observed whenever practical. As a baby learns to help whilst his mother is changing his clothes, each Special Care child should be taught to help in the same way. For example, he should be encouraged to raise an arm, leg or even his back when being dressed – as well as turn his head and other parts of his body. The bigger, or older, child should be taught to use a toilet rather than a potty – to preserve his dignity – and the ambulant child should be encouraged to pull up his own pants when he has finished toileting.

Likewise he should be encouraged to undress: even if he only shakes or pulls his coat off one arm, it is a start! Conversely the hyperactive child may need to be restrained from constantly removing all his articles of clothing!

An excellent book to help the teacher handle the severely physically handicapped child in school is *Handling the Young Cerebral Palsied Child at Home* by Nancy R. Finnie (Heinemann).

Activities for the Special Care child

Child securely harnessed with bare feet in water/sand/lentils/ cardboard box.

Rattles, bells, dolls dangling low over cot or mattress to pull or grasp (some could be on elastic).

Striped plastic curtain strips to look at/walk through/play with.

Child securely placed in hammock *high* in classroom.

Child sitting in sturdy cardboard box with toys (carton gives support and feeling of security).

Barrel for child to be rolled in (and for child to roll toys in – especially *Dinky* cars).

Roll *Dinky* cars down slope.

Roll beach ball, air–flow ball, football towards child.

Play with child in front of mirror – behind him.

Blow up balloon – let him handle it.

Waft paper/cloth in child's face to cause draught.

Blow on him (not in his face – germs).

Humm, buzz, hiss in his ear (make other sounds – see section on making sounds in Chapter 7: Music).

Shine torch in his face, all over his body.

Pull hair, gently.

Swing child in swing.

Slide him down slide.

Play rough and tumble games.

Swing him in air (two adults swing larger child).

Bounce him on trampoline.

Play peek–a–boo.

Hide/show toys and sweets.

Tickle child all over.

Tickle him with a feather, grass, cloth, etc.

Play traditional baby games

    (a) on his hand: 'Round and Round the Garden', and 'There was a Little Mouse';

    (b) with his toes: 'This little Piggy went to Market', and

    (c) clapping games, e.g: 'Clap hands, Daddy comes'.

Play with a musical box.

Play with a jack–in–a–box.

Place tissue paper or thin cloth over child's face, remove saying 'Boo!'.

Place cloth over teacher's face for child to remove.

Hide child's hand/foot in teacher's hands.

Place him in sand, removing socks and shoes. Bury his feet and legs with sand. Trickle sand over his arms, tummy etc.

Sit him in shallow water, trickle water over parts of his body. Give him toys in water (brick, boat, duck, sponge). Splash him gently.

Give him new things to taste, e.g. orange, *Marmite*, flavoured crisps to lick, etc.

Let him handle everything he wants to, making sure it is frequently washed and made of non-toxic material.

Take him out on visits to:
    other Special Care classes
    parks
    teacher's house
    old people's home (with permission).

Share major events with school e.g:
    visitors' concert
    Christmas concert (take part if possible)
    Easter events
    harvest events.

Take whole class into physiotherapy pool, together (one helper needed per child).

Ask physiotherapist what exercises to do daily with each child she sees.

On page 137 is a suggestion for a quick reference chart for each child's needs. The class teacher can adjust the main headings to suit her class but the chart should be kept as brief as possible. It should be displayed in a prominent place in the classroom so that new or relief staff can see instantly what attention each child requires.

The other charts are suggestions for a more comprehensive guide for the teacher to complete every twelve months; and these should be kept with the child's records.

Instant information for staff

	Jane	Janet	Sue	Agnes	Millie	Pete	Bill	John	Sam	Ted
totally immobile										
moves about										
runs away										
good feeder										
special diet										
needs help/persuasion to eat										
sits on potty										
sits on toilet										
inflicts self-injury										
often stubborn										
withdrawn										
home on bus										
home in ambulance										
parents collect										
epileptic										
medication										

Progress and ability chart for a Special Care child

(ideally to be charted every twelve months, kept with child's records)

Name:

Degrees of movement	1978	1979	1980	1981
unable to support head				
can support head				
unable to sit with support				
can sit if supported				
can sit alone				
immobile				
pushes feet against surface				
takes weight on feet				
wriggles				
shuffles				
crawls				
staggers				
walks holding adult's hand				
walks alone				
climbs steps on all fours				
ascends two feet together				
descends two feet together				
ascends alternate feet ⎫ with				
descends alternate feet ⎭ help				
ascends alone				
descends alone				
climbs chairs/tables				
climbs apparatus				
can turn head				
can grip in hand (indicate hand)				
can bend leg (indicate leg)				
can bend arm (indicate arm)				
unaware of dressing				
unable to help dressing				
helps dressing				
takes off coat				
takes off socks				
takes off shoes				

Physical needs	1978	1979	1980	1981
has to be bottle-fed				
can only take liquids				
eats minced food				
requires special diet				
eats adult dinners				
eats biscuits				
eats boiled sweets				
needs spoonfeeding				
holds spoon				
feeds self				
often wets				
often dirty				
sits on potty				
sits on toilet				
occasionally dirty				
occasionally wet				
bowel controlled				
bladder controlled				
toilet trained				
requires medication				

Character
withdrawn
solitary (from choice)
solitary (because of h'cap)
plays near other child
enjoys 'rough and tumble'
sociable
tranquil, happy
dislikes new situations
enjoys new situations
often stubborn
sometimes fretful
temper without tears
cries easily

Degress of intellect	1978	1979	1980	1981
aware of sound				
responds to voice				
responds to own name				
comes when called				
focus on still object for ten seconds				
focus on moving object				
watches other child				
copies other child/adult				
everything to mouth				
everything to eyes				
explores sand				
explores water				
hoards one special object				
hoards many objects				
fondles strange objects				
plays with own body e.g. eyes				
inflicts self-punishment				
reaches for toy				
rattles toy				
holds crayon, brush, etc.				
attempts to clap				
claps hands				
no speech				
single-tone cry				
single-tone laugh				
gurgles				
babble (ka, muh, der)				
two syllables (mama, adah)				
repetitive words				
copies new words				
repetitive phrases				
copies new phrases				
uses sentences				
understands simple commands				

Part 4

Miscellaneous Activities

12　Personal care

Road safety

Road safety is an essential part of the curriculum for the mentally handicapped child. It does not, however, take place as a formal lesson within the school buildings. For an ESNs child to become road-safety conscious, he needs the experience of real traffic in an actual situation.

Police should be brought into the special school as often as possible. The Road Safety Officer will probably have suitable films to show to the child, and the presence of a policeman will emphasize to the child the vital importance of safety on the roads.

However, no film show is a substitute for the real thing. The mentally handicapped child needs to be given daily opportunities of experiencing traffic; he *must* be taught to stop at every kerb – even the narrowest streets are hazardous. He has no inbuilt instinct for danger and needs to learn that cars, buses, lorries and motorbikes are all potentially dangerous and should be regarded with the greatest care. He needs to be made familiar with traffic signals, zebra crossings, the Green Man and the Green Cross Code. Parents of an ordinary child are encouraged not to let the child out on his own until he is five years old. Bearing in mind that a mentally handicapped child may have only a mental age of three years, he needs to be habitually, rigidly and stringently taught, so that crossing a road with due care and attention becomes automatic.

As with the ordinary child, the mentally handicapped child should be instructed not to speak to, accept sweets from, or ride with strangers. The ESNs girl is particularly vulnerable in this respect, as she is often physically normal; but every child should be discouraged from talking to strangers. This can be quite difficult for an ESNs child who may be naturally very friendly and affectionate. Once again, the police will be helpful. The Crime Prevention Officer may well wish to show the older child a film called *Never Go with Strangers*, which is excellent and emphasizes the importance of avoiding any contact with strangers. It is simple but repetitive and is often shown to normal five year olds in their first year at school.

It is also important for the child to know his name and address. He should be taught to say the name of his street *clearly*. If he recites his address automatically and quickly it may not sound clear enough. It is better if he can say the name of his street very clearly, rather than babble his name and full address incoherently.

Below is a rough guide to safety on the roads, with a list of hazards:

Learn the Green Cross Code.
Find a safe place to cross.
Stop at the kerb.
Look all around and listen.
Keep looking and listening when crossing.
Walk quickly – do *not* run.

Use traffic signals and pedestrian lights – pelican crossings.
Red man – STOP.
Green man – GO.
Flashing amber/man – STOP.
Loud bleeping – GO.
Do not cross on zig-zags.
Use zebra crossings or cross to a traffic island.
Beware of parked cars.

A *lollipop man/lady* or a *policeman* will help child cross road safely.
Learn home address.
NEVER speak to strangers.

Hygiene

Hygiene is another subject which is difficult to sit down and teach, but the child needs constant reminders and encouragement to develop clean habits.

He should learn to wash his own hands every time he has been to the toilet; and should also be taught to blow his own nose. Often a mongol child will suffer badly from catarrh and sniff a great deal, so he needs to be taught to use a handkerchief frequently. He should also be discouraged from picking his nose; not only is this unhygienic, but it can damage the delicate membranes inside the nostrils.

Good health and hygiene depend on inner health too, so the mentally handicapped child should be encouraged to eat the correct foods. The older ESNs child often becomes grossly overweight and, despite popular belief, this is usually due to poor eating habits. Sometimes his parents may compensate him by constantly bombarding him with sweets, cakes, biscuits and crisps. It is easy to see his eating habits when he brings food to school for eating at milk-time. Providing each child has had a good breakfast, he should not need any other food until mid-day and teachers should discourage this mid-morning eating habit.

Not only does eating too many sweets and biscuits increase the child's weight, it will also cause tooth decay and bad, decaying teeth will not improve the appearance of any child. He should be encouraged to clean his own teeth, which is difficult to teach in school, but the teacher can talk about it with the class, emphasizing the importance of not eating sweets and paying regular visits to the dentist.

Another task that the ESNs child should learn is to cut his own fingernails. However, it is a rather difficult skill and needs plenty of practice and a good deal of patient teaching. The older girl may find it easier to use an emery board or the boy may prefer to use nail clippers. In any case, his fingernails should be kept short and clean, and therefore every child should be taught to use a nail-brush regularly and scrub his nails clean.

A clean and tidy appearance should also be encouraged and, as the child grows older, he should become conscious of his appearance and want to look tidy. Much of his training in hygiene will come from his parents. Naturally, if they are clean and tidy, their child probably will be too. However, they may be tempted to do it all for him – not thinking to encourage him to help himself become more independent. So the teacher may also need to enlighten the parents in this respect. Below is a list of points for encouraging clean and tidy habits:

Wash hands after using the toilet.
Scrub nails too after painting, modelling, etc.
Blow own nose – don't pick nose or sniff.
Good table manners.

Clean teeth.
Wash own hair.
Bath self.
Girls change own napkin.
Wash small articles of clothing.
Eat correct foods.
Regular visits to dentist.
Cut own fingernails (nail clippers, emery board).
Older girls try using *little* make-up.
Older boys practise shaving with battery shaver.
Clean own shoes.
Boys learn to knot tie.

First aid

All children get cuts and bruises at some time, and the mentally handicapped child is no exception. Indeed, there are additional hazards as he may be overprotected at home, or he may be taking strong drugs which make him clumsy and more likely to fall. A child with epilepsy is particularly vulnerable. Not only are his actual fits worrying, but, with the possibility of an attack at any time, he could injure himself when falling. Most teachers who are experienced in dealing with the ESNS child recognize an epileptic fit and know that there is little to be done, unless the attack lasts more than fifteen minutes, when the doctor or hospital should be informed. The inexperienced may find the fit disturbing at first and the more experienced teacher should try to be reassuring.

Due to the nature of his disability, the ESNS child is often prescribed regular medication. Any medicines he needs to have in school should be locked in a cabinet or drawer and the key made available to the staff, well out of the child's reach. Lists of each child's medication should be regularly checked, as medicines are often changed or discontinued. These lists should include the amounts to be taken in grammes or millilitres.

Every classroom should have a small first-aid box, containing assorted plasters, cotton-wool, lint, antiseptic ointment and witch-hazel (which is excellent for reducing the swelling of bruises). If any child scalds or burns himself then the burnt area should be immediately immersed in cold water until the redness has lessened. It should then be covered *lightly* with a piece of lint. All disinfectants and tablets should be kept locked in a safe place, such as the medical room (if the school is lucky enough to have one) or the staff room. The child should be made aware of the danger of poisons such as those contained in disinfectant bottles. He should not be encouraged to play with these bottles, even if they are washed, clean and empty, for the phrase 'familiarity breeds contempt' is very apt in this situation.

Disinfectant should, however, be used in the classrooms, particularly at the younger end of the school. All toys, potties, tables, chairs and other equipment should be washed with diluted disinfectant at least on a weekly basis, as the child in these classes probably has no bladder control and maybe no bowel control either. Unfortunately he sometimes has to eat in the same surroundings, so the teacher and her assistants must be certain that both they themselves and the equipment are scrupulously clean.

Below is a short list of suggested items for first-aid boxes:

1 In the classroom:

Ready-cut plaster	lint
strip plaster	witch-hazel
cotton-wool	eye-wash
cotton-buds	eye-bath
antiseptic cream	tweezers
small, sharp scissors	olive oil

2 In school:

junior asprins	oil of cloves
disinfectant	antiseptic medical wipes
liquid antiseptic	thermometer
bandages	teaspoon
sterilized dressings	bowls
sling	cotton-wool
antiseptic cream	lint
calomine lotion	gauze
antihistamine cream	boracic powder
mouthwash	elastic bandages
zinc and castor oil	tissues
sanitary towels	hot-water-bottle
surgical spirit	oil of peppermint
safety pins	bicarbonate of soda
medicine glass	notebook for list of injuries

Suggested treatment for likely incidents

Bites and stings
Remove sting with tweezers, apply antihistamine cream.

Bleeding from nose
Pinch area just above hard part of nose, sit child upright in current of air. If persistent, take to doctor or hospital. Do not plug or blow nose.

Bruises
Swelling may be reduced with quick application of witch-hazel.

Burns
Instantly immerse in cold water. If mouth or throat is scalded suck ice cubes.

Foreign body
May be in eye, ear, nose or throat. Do not probe! Give eye-wash or 'blow' on child's back as required. Take to doctor or hospital (casualty department).

Grazes
Remove any visible foreign bodies, clean with cotton-wool or lint and liquid antiseptic. Cover with plaster or bandage.

Headache
Lie child down in dark room if possible, induce sleep. If a child frequently complains of headaches, is he suffering from eye strain?

Heat exhaustion
Place in cool, darkened room, give child plenty of liquids. (Add half a teaspoonful of salt to every pint – it may be the loss of salt through perspiration that has made the child exhausted.)

Sickness
If child is pale, clammy and starts to cough and retch, remove him from the group, loosen clothing, ensure good air supply, sit or lie child down.

If a number of children suffer, preserve and cover a specimen and, if possible, obtain sample of food eaten. Inform local health authority and doctor.

Splinters
Remove with tweezers or use a needle dipped in boiling water or passed through a flame. Bathe with liquid antiseptic.

Toothache
Dip cotton-bud into oil of cloves, place on infected area. Inform dentist.

'Tummy-ache'
Unfasten tight clothing. Apply hot-water-bottle. Give child warm water to drink containing two or three drops of oil of peppermint in medicine glass. Severe pain or vomiting should be reported to the doctor.

13 Storytelling and visual aids

Stories are very popular with the mentally handicapped child and he loves to hear favourite stories again and again. Naturally there is an art in telling stories, but it is not a difficult art to achieve. After all, most parents become storytellers at some time, and every child's imagination is stimulated by fairy tales and stories of beautiful princesses with their handsome and charming princes!

There are two facets of storytelling which are of paramount importance: first, a good storybook containing clear, colourful pictures, and second, the storyteller should know the story fairly well, so that she doesn't need to read it word by word. The teacher can introduce new stories fairly frequently, and colourful friezes or collages can be created by the class who enjoyed the story. The older child should be able to follow a simple serial, told in short periods over a week or fortnight. For instance, he will probably thoroughly enjoy a good adventure story. He could possibly even act it out in a follow-up drama session.

Visual aids go hand-in-hand with storytelling. Every story needs good, big, colourful pictures to bring it to life, and the teacher should try to acquire many varied pictures from magazines or storybooks, and she could even make some herself. There should be a book corner in most classrooms where the child can go and look at storybooks and even 'read' them to himself or a friend.

Colourful wall charts are not, however, true visual aids unless they are well used, helping the teacher to teach and the child to learn. Colourful pictures are not only useful, they brighten up the classroom too, and every subject the child learns will be more interesting if there are bright pictures on the classroom walls for him to see and learn from. Cookery charts are an obvious example, giving step-by-step illustrations of the current cookery session. There could also be illustrations of nature sessions, music, PE, movement and so on.

Some special schools are lucky enough to have audio-visual

equipment or 'hardware' as it is fashionably called: this term simply includes tape recorders, various projectors and cameras, record players and other similar equipment, under the one heading.

Much of this equipment, like the overhead projector which is effective in daylight, is very useful and enables the teacher to create her own illustrations. Special sheets and markers are provided and the teacher can make permanent illustrations or simply wash off ones she no longer needs.

Large 16mm sound projectors are also helpful, but rather expensive, especially if there are no films available on free loan from the local education authority's resource centre. All cameras are, however, extremely useful and the teacher can use them to make her own visual aids or to keep a record of the school's many activities. The interested teacher could make or acquire a set of visual aids in the form of 35mm slides for the school to catalogue and keep. For example, a good series of pictures of water could be collected, showing the differences between the sea, a lake, canal and river; or a series of different buildings of, perhaps, a house, skyscraper, church and factory. The child could learn a great deal from such slides, even if he has never actually seen the sea, a canal, or a factory. If he has been on suitable visits then the slides will reinforce his experiences and later jog his memory.

A list of various visual aids follows, which, it is hoped, will be of some help to teachers when seeking the most useful purchases.

Audio-visual chart

Cameras	Uses and advantages	Disadvantages
Instamatic	Films easy to load; flash convenient; automatic light settings; fixed focus.	Average quality prints. Close-ups will not focus.
35mm	Excellent quality photos for visual aids. Slides can be projected and produce excellent pictures.	Must be used by experienced person. Films can be difficult to load. May have complicated settings.
Polaroid	Instant pictures.	Films very expensive. If mistimed, photo ruined.
16mm cine	Too expensive and unsuitable.	

8mm cine	Moving record of school events. Super 8, larger picture than standard 8. Let subject move – do not move camera.	Films expensive, school needs projector too, for full benefit.

Projectors	*Uses and advantages*	*Disadvantages*
Overhead	Can be used in daylight. Teacher makes own visual aid with special pen. Can be erased and reused like a blackboard. Teacher faces class.	Teacher in an ESNs school rarely needs to use a blackboard.
35mm slide	Shows good slides, sequence can be re-arranged to emphasize different aspect. Can be used with tape-recorded commentary. Often has remote controls.	Needs darkened room. Takes time to pre-load slides in magazine or circular tray.
Film strip	Keeps pictures in sequence in small tube. Small storage space. Attachment must be used on 35mm projector.	Extra cost for slides to be made into strips. If borrowed, strips may get badly scratched. Sequence cannot be changed.
Super 8mm	Pleasant record of school's activities, for example Sports Day. Can show films to outside audience.	Needs darkened room. Silent film track often quite short, but films can be spliced together.
16mm sound, cine	Good visual aid if film on relevant topic is available. Search for free-loan films from industrial firms.	Heavy to carry. Expensive to buy. Needs darkened room. Noise may be distracting.
8mm film loop	Easy to use. Can make own commentary. Colour, moving pictures in cassettes, continuous running.	Has a small screen i.e. not projected onto large screen; only suitable for small groups.

Episcope	Will project pictures from books, magazines, etc. Can be used in daylight.	Only projects pictures up to 5" square.
Epidiascope	Projects larger pictures from books, magazines, etc.	Very heavy to carry. Expensive.

All films and slides show better on a good-quality white screen.

Tape recorders	*Uses and advantages*	*Disadvantages*
Tapes	Loose tape-ribbon on machine. Easily spliced if broken.	Not child-proof! Awkward to thread. Ribbon easily damaged.
Cassettes	Enclosed tape-ribbon. Easy to load, easy to use. Child less able to damage tape.	Not easy to find marked place on tape.
Cartridges	Easy to use, as cassettes.	Tape cannot be rewound.

Other visual aids		
Flannelgraph	Large backcloth with assorted pictures which adhere to it as required.	May lose clinging quality after frequent use.
Magnetic board	Large metal board. Wood or card models can be moved about by means of small magnets attached.	More expensive than above to set up.

14 Timetables and play activities

Making a timetable for the whole school is one of the headteacher's most awkward tasks. She has to account for every eventuality, making certain that each class has enough time in the gym or use of the hall, that TV and radio are available at the relevant times, that dinner times are sufficiently covered and, most of all, that each teacher is, as far as possible, able to have the timetable she wishes. There is an amazing amount of organization necessary if, for example, there is only one television set. The headteacher needs to be certain all classes have the opportunity to see their relevant programmes. She has to arrange for either the TV to be moved to the classroom, or the class to go to the television: if the latter case, the class in the room with the TV will need accommodating elsewhere.

Visits can also be a nuisance if they disturb the timetables, but every class needs at least one a week. Very often the headteacher needs to make certain enough help is available for outings – for example, the Special Care class may need extra help to push the wheel-chairs.

Therefore, special and regular events need to be taken into account. For instance, how many staff go swimming, how often, and are their classes catered for? Many ESNs schools now have a minibus, thanks to the Variety Club of Great Britain and other charitable organizations, so the headteacher needs to find a capable driver. Some schools are lucky enough to employ a 'handyman' who also drives the minibus. The alternative is to make use of every teacher who drives and create a 'minibus rota' enabling every class to have regular minibus outings.

However, timetables are not essential just for the smooth running of the school; they are also important for the development of the child. He needs to learn a routine and will probably be unable to develop fully in a haphazard situation. His ability to remember the routine daily activities will be reinforced if his parents are given a copy of his timetable. This will enable them to discuss relevant activities with him and thus his understanding will develop more fully.

Variety is necessary within the routine, however, and each teacher should try to create an interesting and varied timetable for her class. The older child could be made more aware of his timetable if a representational one is displayed on the classroom wall. This could provide a regular and interesting discussion topic for the class.

The relevance of timetables has also been discussed in Chapter 2: The child's needs, and each teacher likes to create her own timetable to suit her needs, in addition to her class's needs. However, as the child develops through the school, his needs develop too, and so his timetable should develop. Examples of different types of activities for his timetable are listed below.

Basic play is vital in the development of the ESNs child and it is expected that most teachers and students understand the child's need to discover through play. Therefore a list of interesting play activities for the young and older mentally handicapped child is also included.

Timetable activities

(a) *For the younger child*

singing

music

storytelling

painting

climbing activities

visit

small activities (bean bag, ball, etc.)

simple cookery

tidy up

free play;

free choice; guided activities; free activities (according to individual teacher, but daily sessions of assorted activities are essential)

(b) *For the older child* (in addition to those mentioned above)

discussions

nature

cookery

sports

PE

music and movement

homecrafts

handicrafts

TV

radio

films, slides, etc.

swimming

creative activities

Hints about routine activities

(a) *For the younger child* (up to 7 years)

Assuming every child is mobile, the inexperienced or student teacher may need a few hints about teaching routine activities:

1 The child should never be lifted down from the coach – steps are important for rhythm and balance, and there may be no steps in school.

2 The child should be allowed to remove his own coat and hat, and helped to identify his own peg. His name and/or a picture should be glued next to his peg.

3 His teacher could sing while washing his hands – 'This is the way we wash your hands', for example.

4 When washing and drying a child's hands, the teacher should stand behind the child, making the correct movements; providing the child can see his teacher through the mirror, and hear her voice, he will not be nervous.

5 Each child, in turn, should be taught to pour the milk, or put a straw in each bottle, and help to wash the beakers after milk.

6 For a talking point, the teacher of the very young child should keep it simple; just discuss a child's birthday and notice if any child is absent.

7 Singing should not last more than five minutes for the very young, unless the group has good concentration.

8 Songs are the beginnings of a directed social situation and will increase the child's confidence even if he has to learn them by rote.

9 Finger games and action songs are also social activities, and help him develop muscle control.

10 The class should be very close to the teacher, so that the children can see her face more clearly, and she will be able to help each child's actions.

11 Stories should be told with many bright, large, clear pictures, or the teacher could provide a storybox, which contains items from the story, like a teddy-bear, or a little red train.

12 Repetitive stories with a refrain for the child to join in are popular too.

Table games:

1 Nesting boxes, tins: Useful for building towers and knocking them down, learning about size, colour and shape, fitting them together, playing in the water or sand, making a noise (bang two together or place small one inside larger one and rattle them), hiding small under large.

2 Locking bricks, e.g. *Nursery Lego*: Useful for hand/eye coordination, can be placed in a long line, a wide line, made to 'fence' something in, or built high one on top of the other.

3 Lightweight large bricks: Useful for building up, knocking down, building a wall, making three sides of a square to crawl into, building a bed, a chair, a road or a railway, and a bridge over the road.

(b) *For the older child* (7–13 years)
1 He should be able to leave the coach by himself – but may still need help in identifying his coat peg, particularly by name.
2 He may still have difficulty in fastening press-studs or zips, but will probably be able to unfasten them.
3 He will probably need supervision in the toilet, but generally he should be able to manage by himself.
4 At milk-time the teacher will still need to help him pour, but he should be able to learn which child has milk and who has a different drink (one child may be on a special diet, for instance).
5 Discussions should last longer and he should be able to talk about his activities last night, his favourite TV programme or having a new dress/pair of shoes, for instance.
6 The singing session should be longer and he ought to be able to choose some songs he wants to sing.
7 The teacher should provide stories with more detail and a slightly more involved plot.
8 Made-up stories about the child's own interests and activities will be popular, more so if they could be illustrated with photographs taken on the occasion.

Table games:
1 Concerned with shape. Jigsaws, posting boxes, fitting assorted shapes into correct holes, inset boards and form boards – good for hand/eye coordination, manipulation and helps child learn concept of shape.
2 Threading toys and threading beads – again helps hand/eye coordination and manipulation. Can also help colour, and the beginnings of patterns, e.g. two red beads, one blue, two red, etc.
3 Sorting boxes; to do with colour, shape and, maybe, number – for instance, red pegs into red holes, box number 5 requires five objects.
4 Matching domino-type cards, matching numbers, pictures and some words; solitary game or social game.
5 Plays simple table games *with friends*. For example, using a coloured dice, when he rolls it to red, he picks up a red counter. His friend rolls the dice, perhaps to blue, and picks up a blue

counter. It is a social game, yet each child has to learn to wait his turn, and know that when the set of red counters has gone he can only have a counter of a different colour. Therefore if he rolls a red dice he misses a turn.

6   Assembles construction toys, plastic nuts and bolts, wooden frames. Metal *Meccano* sets are too small for him, but he can make recognizable objects with the plastic sets, like aeroplanes, windmills.

7   Can build 'houses' with small locking bricks like *Lego*; can make a pattern with them – two white, three red, two white, for example.

(c)   *For the teenager* (13–16 years)

1   Most should be trusted to use the toilets by themselves: boys should be taught to stand at the urinal, if the school has one. Girls should be taught to change their own napkin regularly during menstruation.

2   The teacher should encourage the child to *want* to look neat and tidy – boys should see that their shirts are tucked in and ties straight and girls should ensure that their tights are not wrinkled or their petticoats showing.

3   Girls should be taught to sit with their legs together.

4   Each child should be able to dress and undress for PE with the minimum of trouble.

5   Encourage the child's parents to buy shoes *without* laces if possible, so that he doesn't need to learn how to fasten them.

6   There could possibly be a milk-table or milk-bar for him to drink his milk from whenever he wishes, providing he washes his own beaker/bottle when he has finished.

7   The teacher could guide the class's discussions, which should include current affairs, such as a Royal Wedding or the Olympics, and discuss various festivals celebrated throughout the year – Easter, Christmas, Hallowe'en and Mother's Day, for example.

Table games:

1   More sophisticated, requiring the teenage mentally handicapped child to actually *do* and *think* more. For example, he should have his own workbook for copying shapes or practising writing.

2   Money dominoes: matching 1p to a penny coin, 1p to 1p, or coin to coin. Child should become familiar with money and be encouraged to recognize it written down as a price and as a coin.

3   Picture and word games. There are many different types of these,

but essentially the child should learn to match word for word, letter for letter, picture to word (in a jigsaw first) and lastly place a missing letter into a word. The words and pictures should, of course, be simple (such as sun, pig, bus, dog, hat, etc.).

4   Football number game – between two. Each child has a stack of 'footballs' (flat discs, striped on one side, numbered on the other). A board is divided into two, each side having assorted numbers in circles. Child turns up 'football' disc in turn and covers up the same number on the board – as in Bingo. Child who covers all his numbers first wins.

5   Able to use more complicated construction toys, may be able to copy a construction.

Play activities

1   *Wendy house* with cooker, dolls, cupboard, cups and saucers, curtains, carpet, table, stool, chair, bed, cot, empty tins.

2   *Shop* with empty tins (make sure there are no sharp edges!), apron, pretend cakes, bread and pies, empty cartons of food. (Make shop variable, e.g. bookshop, toyshop, clothes shop.)

3   *Dough or pastry play* (see recipe – page 58). All colours, use rolling pin, pastry cutters, oddments to make impressions.

4   *Water play* with or without bubbles; pipes, tubes, cones, tubs, sponge, sieve, colander, funnel, boat, cork, stones.

5   *Sand play* with wet or dry sand, spade, bucket, sieve, colander, comb, brush, funnel, scoop.

6   *Large, moving toys* – tricycles, push and pull toys, prams, rocking horses, wheelbarrow, double rockers. Large carton full of assorted tins (no sharp edges). Large box full of assorted tubes and cartons.

7   *Colour table* with everything on table (and wall behind) of the same colour.

8   *Interest table* where old clocks, radios, watches, photographs, etc. can be displayed.

9   *Puppet theatre* – puppets on sticks, hand puppets, sock puppets, animal and human puppets. Use sturdy card box with curtains.

Every teacher will probably have a few moments to spare during the day. Maybe the school dinner is a little late, or a particular lesson is not going as well as was planned – even the best organization can go awry! It is for these sometimes embarrassing moments that the following list of 'Five-minute fill-ins' has been devised.

Five-minute fill-ins

Doing
Wiggle each finger in turn.
Pull funny faces.
Make frightening faces.
Pick up pencil with toes.
Pick up pencil from table with lips (one pencil each).
Wiggle nose, ears, eyebrows, jaw.
Make funny noises; use fingers and lips.
Make frightening noises.
Who can hold breath the longest?

Talking
Talk about and feel *bones*.
Teacher describes a child, class guess who it is.
Teacher describes an object (seen or unseen), class guesses the object.
Record chatter with class, play it back − fast, slow.
What's missing? Memory game.
Think of TV advertisements and sing some.
Make up rhyming words about class, for example: 'I know a boy whose name is John, Who went to bed with his tee-shirt on!'
Name different animals; fruits; vegetables; meat; flowers; sweets; TV heroes; pop stars, etc.
I-spy game, for example: 'I spy with my little eye, Something ... (blue) *or* Something beginning with ... (colour or sound, not the letter).'
General guessing game, for example: What flies in the air? What swims? What walks? Wriggles? etc.

More comprehensive lists of activities for mentally handicapped children of all ages can be found in *The Educational and Social Needs of Children with Severe Handicap* by Mildred Stevens (Arnold 1976) and *Observe − Then Teach* by Mildred Stevens (Arnold 1978).

15 Classroom testing

The value and importance of regularly testing the mentally handicapped child cannot be overemphasized. There are many different professions who are interested in testing him, but they often devise their own very complicated and intricate tests which may require as long as an hour or even a full day to test one child. This is totally impractical for the teacher, who needs to know in which areas the child is weakest. If she is told that he achieved a score of 28 per cent or .7 on a particular scale, she has no idea how the child attained that figure, even though she may know the kind of test that was used. Therefore it is more practical for her to devise her own tests to suit her class to enable her to make her own regular assessment.

There are many more reasons for regularly testing the mentally handicapped child. Initially they provide the teacher or student with something interesting to do on first meeting an ESNs child, while at the same time illustrating each child's weakest areas of development: for example, does he need help with manipulative skills like cutting or threading, or does he require more intellectual help with counting and number?

The difference between a test and other individual teaching activities are the conditions. It would, no doubt, be a more accurate and precise test if teacher and child were totally isolated from any other stimulus. However, the new surroundings may overawe the child, who may then be unable to relax sufficiently to take part in the test. It is much more practical for the teacher to find a quiet corner in the classroom where she could test the child. For this reason the test should not be prolonged; the child may not be able to concentrate for a long period with other activities going on around him. The teacher should simply concentrate on testing certain skills, like matching pictures or sorting colours. She should not, for example, try to test his social behaviour or his abilities in self-help; instead she should be continually observing these abilities in school and conscientiously record her observations.

When testing, it is important to give the same instructions to each child in the same way, preferably using gestures and words. The results need to be carefully and accurately recorded so that the teacher has a clear comparison next time the child is tested, say in three or six months' time. The testing material could be kept specifically for testing, but the child can be encouraged to use and play with similar material in the classroom. It is a good idea to write down the instructions for the tests, not only to remind the teacher, but also so that she can pass the tests on to another member of staff who may be having that class or who may simply be interested.

A list of various tests follows. Some are suitable for the younger child, some for the older child, while some are simply ideas for recording the teacher's own observations about each child's needs.

The teacher is not expected to test each child on everything in the lists, but it is hoped that she will derive ideas for a number of relevant tests.

Intellectual tests A

No language required from the child

1   *Recognition*
Is child aware of:
(a) sounds − soft? loud? high? deep?
(b) position of sound − up or down?
Does child respond to 'No' or loud voice?
Does child respond to own name, as opposed to other child's name?

Will child show required objects? For example: 'Show me the ball.' or 'Where is the ball?' Suggestions for other objects − doll, shoe, comb, cup, spoon, hat. If child gestures, for example points to own foot for 'shoe', then it is clear he understands 'shoe' and should be marked accordingly.

Is he able to pick out shapes in the same way? For instance: 'Show me the circle.'; 'Give me the square.'; 'Where is the triangle?' The teacher should use each kind of sentence until she is sure the child is unable to do what is required; she can then assess his ability.

2   *Sorting*
Odd one out: 'Find me the odd man out.'; 'Which does not belong?'; 'Which one is different?' or 'Show me the odd one.' With practice the teacher will be able to choose the most appropriate sentence.

Suggested oddities:
car amongst bricks
spoon amongst beads
round bead amongst bricks
red brick amongst blue ones
sort big from little
thick from thin
red from blue (and other colours)
circles from squares (and other shapes).

Later this can be taken further so that the child is asked to: 'Find the red square.' And then 'Find the thin, red square.' And so on with more elaborate requests.

3 Matching

Suggestions: 'Find me one the same as this.' (Teacher holds up a car, brick, colour, shape or picture, etc.) or 'Give me another one the same.' or 'Which looks the same?'

In the earliest stage of matching it is important that the child has to choose identical objects. In many ways it may be easier for the teacher to make up a set of her own pictures. For example, she could use advertisements in magazines. If these are cut out, pasted on to card and covered with clear cellophane, they will last for many years and be a helpful testing aid.

One of the most useful pieces of apparatus which can be bought is *Attribute Blocks* by Invicta, which are tough plastic assorted shapes in three bright colours, red, blue and yellow, some small, some large, some thick and some thin. These are rather expensive, but good value as every teacher throughout the school should find some use for them.

4 Understanding number

The testing of the understanding of number is not very easy, particularly with the mentally handicapped child. He may know the meaning of few and many, but may not be able to understand it during the conditions of the test. Once again the teacher must use her own judgment, but beware of trying to *make* the child show right answer.

One early test, according to Piaget, of the child understanding number is 'one-to-one correspondence'. This simply means that the child can match one teaspoon per cup or one straw per milk bottle, and so on. This can be tested by the teacher saying: 'Give every bottle a straw.' or 'Put a teaspoon in every cup.' When the child is able to do this correctly he should begin to learn 'more' and 'less'. For example, if two cups are provided and ten teaspoons, then there are *more* teaspoons.

A recommended book on number is *Mathematics Begins* a Nuffield Mathematics Project (W. & R. Chambers and John Murray 1967 for the Schools Council). It covers matching, sorting and other early number activities.

5   *Sequencing*

This is also quite difficult to test, and the teacher will probably have to make her own sequencing cards. For example, pictures of:

(a) a tiny shoot growing out of the soil
(b) the same shoot growing taller
(c) the same shoot with two leaves
(d) the same shoot − very large now with many leaves
(e) the same shoot with a large flower as well as the leaves.

The child should be asked, 'Which picture is first?' or 'What comes first?'

Here is another suggestion:

(a) the foundations of a house being built
(b) the same house with a little wall and window frames
(c) bricks continued above the window frames
(d) the door and roof on the house
(e) the finished house with curtains, smoke from chimney, path to door and garden.

Even with this kind of sequence of pictures the child may not understand what is required, and may choose the last picture first because he likes it, or because it is 'complete'.

6   *Time*

There are several ways of testing the child's knowledge of time without requiring him to speak. For example:

'Was it Monday yesterday?'
'Will it be Thursday tomorrow?'
'Is three o'clock dinner-time?'
'Show me the clock.'
'Where is my watch?'

If the teacher has some prepared clock faces with times on, such as 12 o'clock, 4.30, 6 o'clock and 8.30 she could test the child more easily. For instance: 'Show me tea-time.'; 'Show me dinner-time.' and so on, including bed-time and time to get up.

The teacher could also use these cards to test the child's actual knowledge of time. For example: 'Where is ten o'clock?' or 'Which one says half past four?' and so on.

Another useful piece of apparatus is the open clock face. The teacher could ask the child: 'Show me 11 o'clock.' or 'What does 3 o'clock look like?', and hopefully the child will move the fingers accordingly.

Whether it is relevant or not for the mentally handicapped child to learn how to tell the time is a controversial subject, but this section has been included for those teachers who feel that it is relevant.

7 Understanding language

This is more easy to test, as the equipment can be kept to a minimum and very simple.

For instance, the teacher needs only a small brick and a beaker for the following instructions:

'Put the brick in (into, inside) the beaker.'
'Put the beaker over (on top of) the brick.'
or 'Cover the brick with the beaker.'
or 'Put the brick inside the beaker.'
'Put the brick upon the beaker.'
'Put the brick in front of the beaker.'
'Put the brick behind the beaker.'
'Put the brick on the chair.'
'Give me the beaker.' (without holding out hand)

In fact, all the tests previously listed test the child's understanding of language too.

More useful words to test:

inside	open	sit down
outside	close	upstairs
between	stand up	downstairs
beside		

Intellectual tests B

In addition to the above mentioned but *requiring language from the child*.

1 Recognition

His vocabulary could be tested with a series of pictures. These may be cut out from magazines or very clearly drawn, pasted on card and covered with cellophane. The child's response should be very carefully recorded. For example, he may say: 'night'; 'moon'; 'dark'; 'stars', or 'sleep' for a picture of the dark, night sky. He may even say 'moon' if he is shown a picture of a sunset. The child's answers, therefore, are neither right nor wrong – and need no score – but his answer should be written down to compare it with next time, and to keep as a record of his growing vocabulary. The school could even have printed sheets of the lists with spaces for the child's comments.

Some suggested pictures:

apple	dinner	moon
baby	door	orange
ball	egg	queen
banana	fire	policeman
bat	flower	sea
bed	girl	shoe
boat	hand	spoon
boy	handbag	sun
bus	hat	sweets
car	hen	table
chair	horse	tap
children	house	teapot
clock	king	toys
coins	man	train
cot	men	TV
cow	milk	water
cup	money	woman

Pictures provide a different medium for the child to relate to (as opposed to real objects like chair, spoon). It is also easier for the teacher, as she can keep the pictures neatly together in a comparatively small space.

2   *Memory*

The ESNs child has a notoriously poor memory and the teacher is constantly trying to improve it. Initially he will learn things by rote; unfortunately, he is often unable to chant a song or rhyme on request, so the teacher will have to use her own observations. As he grows older, however, she will be able to test his retaining powers.

Suggestions:
'Sing your favourite song for me.' (4 lines)
'Do you know the days of the week?'
'Do you know the months of the year?'
'When is your birthday?'
'What is your name and address?'
'Where do you live?'

Say a short sentence to the child, ask him to repeat it. Try a longer one if he's successful. For instance:

'Robert went to bed.'

'Robert went to bed yesterday.'

'Robert went to bed at 10 o'clock yesterday.'

and so on.

3   Use of language

Much of this too needs to be carefully observed and recorded in the classroom, but if the opportunity arises the teacher could test the child's use of language. Usually the most profitable way is to persuade him to talk about his family (parents, brothers, sisters), and any pets or interests he may have.

Suggestions:

'Does your Dad go to work?'

'Does your Mum go to work?'

'Does your brother/sister go to school?'

'Which school?'

'What does your dog/rabbit eat?'

'Have you got a garden?'

'What toys have you got at home?'

'What is your favourite song/record?'

'Who is your favourite pop singer?'

'What do you like on television?'

The child's responses should be recorded, not necessarily in detail, but the approximate quality of his language should be observed. For example:

monosyllables	very talkative
two words	giggly
phrases	incoherent
short sentences	long sentences

4   Word recognition

Sometimes an ESNs child has a knack for remembering written words. He may begin by repeating certain words constantly and later be able to read simple words. For the older child it is important that he learns what is known as a 'social sight' vocabulary. For whatever reason, the mentally handicapped should be made familiar with words; they are a natural part of everyday life and cannot be ignored, even though he may never be able to read.

'*Social sight words*' sometimes referred to as *social mobility*:

On	No Entry	Vacant
Off	No Admittance	*Engaged*
Press	*Private*	*Poison*
Ring	Prohibited	*Ladies*
Push	Keep Out	*Gentlemen*
Pull	Keep Off	*Gents*
Stop	*Toilet*	Men
Cross Now	Lavatory	Women
Cross Here	Public Convenience	Police
Entrance		

The most important or most common are italicized.

Other words that the mentally handicapped child may recognize are:

his own name

his friends' names

his surname

some words in the classroom

some words in a reading book.

He may be familiar with popular shop names, e.g. Boots, Woolworth, Marks and Spencer, C & A, British Home Stores or Mothercare. He may know the name of his own local shop or the Post Office.

5   *Number*

Child says a few numbers, not in order.

Child counts by rote to five.

Child counts by rote to ten.

Child counts three objects.

Child counts five or more objects.

Child counts assorted articles.

Child groups together selected number of objects from larger number.

Child recognizes written numbers.

Child picks out any written number up to ten.

Child understands that five cars is *more than* three cars.

6   *Sequencing*

Even though the child is able to speak quite coherently, it is difficult to test his understanding of sequence and the order of events. The teacher can ask questions such as:

'What is the first thing you do in the morning?'

'What do you do after you get off the school coach?'

'Who gets *on* the coach *after* you in the morning?'

'Who gets *off* the coach *before* you in the afternoon?'

'What happens in school after you've hung up your hat and coat?' The questions seem rather long and complicated, but it is no use expecting the child to understand a sequence of events that he has never experienced. Here is a usual sequence which he may regularly experience:

Getting up	1	gets out of bed
	2	washes
	3	dresses
	4	breakfasts
	5	puts on coat
	6	goes out

However, the child may say that the first thing he does is have breakfast – never assume he is wrong, he *may* have breakfast in bed!

7   *Time*

Many ways of testing the child's knowledge and understanding of time have been described earlier in this chapter. However, he can also be tested by using his own language. For example:

'What time do you go to bed?'

'What time do you have tea?'

'What time do you get up?'

He may even be able to tell the time by the hour, or tell the teacher what time the next lesson is due!

Physical skills

Manipulation

Has the child a firm grip?

Can he pick up a large object?

Can he pick up a small object?

Can he pick up cotton?

Does he use his first finger and thumb?

Can he build a two-brick tower?

Can he turn pages of a book?

Can he turn one page at a time?

Cutting

Can he hold the scissors correctly?

Can he cut?

Can he make several snips?

Can he cut in a straight line?
Can he cut along a wavy line?
Can he cut out a picture?
Can he cut a star shape?
Can he cut material?

Drawing
Can he hold a pencil or crayon?
Can he hold it correctly?
Can he scribble?
Can he cover the paper with scribble?
Can he draw circles?
Can he draw recognizable shapes?
Can he draw people?
Can he copy shapes?
Can he draw imaginary animals?
Can he draw an object by copying it? (Goodenough's *Draw a Man Test* (Harris 1963) is an excellent guide.)

Hand/eye coordination

Threading
Can he put beads on to sticks?
Can he thread with toy (i.e. a *Threading Block*, made by Aarikka, which has a stick on a rope to push through holes)?
Can he thread lace through a hole?
Can he thread beads with a shoelace?
Can he push a needle through the holes in a sewing card?
Can he thread a large-eyed needle?
Can he thread a small-eyed needle with cotton?

Patterns
Can he fit pegs into holes?
Can he copy a pattern of pegs from a card?
Can he copy a pattern of threading beads from a card?
Can he copy a simple shape (e.g. circle, square, triangle)?
Can he copy more complex shapes (e.g. star, circle inside square, square on top of plus sign)?

Following lines
Can he follow a single line with his fingers?
Can he push a car along a wide double track?

Can he do it without letting the car touch the sides?
Can he make the car follow a more bendy track?
Can he make the car follow a narrow track?
Can he trace his finger around a shape (square, circle, triangle)?
Can he trace a more complex shape (e.g. star) with his finger?
Can he use tracing paper?
Can he draw a simple shape with tracing paper?
Can he draw a more complex shape with tracing paper?
Can he use a template?
Can he use a template which has not been fixed into position?

Teacher's own observations
(For the Special Care Child, see pages 138–40 inclusive.)

Physical skills
Does he walk clumsily?
Does he walk steadily?
Can he run?
Can he skip?
Can he hop?
Can he stride over low apparatus?
Can he climb on to low apparatus?
Is he adventurous at climbing?
Can he pedal a three-wheeled bike?
Can he ride a two-wheeled bike?
Can he use roller-skates, stilts or any other similar apparatus?

Self help
Is his bowel controlled?
Is his bladder controlled?
Is he toilet-trained?
Can he pull up his own pants after using the toilet?
Can he turn on the taps?
Can he put the plug in?
Can he wash his own hands?
Can he dry his own hands?
Can he take off his shoes?
Can he take off his socks?
Can he take off his coat?
Can he put on his shoes – socks – coat?
Does he like to look neat and tidy?
Does he know to take off his jumper/cardigan in hot weather?

Does he know to put on his jumper/cardigan in cold weather?
Does he eat with a spoon?
Does he eat with a spoon and fork?
Does he use a knife and fork?
Can he eat an apple, and leave the core?
Can he peel, then eat, a banana?

Character

Friendly towards staff.	Shuns new experiences.
Friendly towards strangers.	Uncooperative.
Sociable with friends.	Stubborn.
Kind to friends.	Aggressive.
Enjoys new experiences.	Withdrawn.
Generally cooperative.	Cries easily.
Overaffectionate.	Often becomes frustrated.
Easily distracted.	Has occasional tantrums.
Timid, shy.	Has frequent bad tempers.
Only shy with strangers.	Bullies his friends.

The ideas for some of the above tests have come from Piaget, Frostig, Gunzberg, and Mary Sheridan's *Developmental Chart for the Progress of Infants and Young Children* (published by HMSO).

The Goodenough *Draw a Man Test* can be found in *Children's Drawings as Measures of Intellectual Ability* by D. B. Harris (Harcourt, Brace and World; New York 1963).

Part 5

Themes

16   Themes

Themes are of major importance in the classroom and the teacher devotes much of her time to devising those which will suit her class. For example, if the theme is 'Water', she may arrange for the class to visit the seaside, a lake or river, help them make an indoor pond, select suitable aquatic life for music and movement, seek out watery stories, songs and so on. Many other themes involve shape, colour and number, and will help the child develop an awareness of his immediate environment if sufficiently emphasized by his teacher.

However, she should not rely on these themes alone for it can happen that for a month, or possibly longer, the child is intensely aware of everything to do with 'Buildings', for example. Then, as the theme is changed he completely forgets all about 'Buildings' and concentrates on 'Fruit'. One of the teacher's tasks is to help him retain information on one theme whilst absorbing facts about another. This is possibly one of the most difficult aspects of teaching the ESNs child, but again, perseverance and determination on the teacher's part should be worth while.

A list of fifty themes has been devised, which includes suggestions for discussion points, songs and suitable visits and a comprehensive range of art work. Naturally some themes will last longer than others: for example, 'Transport' has a much wider scope than 'Africa', but all, it is hoped, will be of some use to the teacher.

Africa

Points for discussion

wild animals	carved animals	nomad
jungle	tree house	tribe
Tarzan	desert	hunter
natives	hot sun	cannibals
mud huts	oasis	cooking pot
canoe	palm trees	spears
colourful beads	caravan (camels)	

Interesting words

safari   witchdoctor   swamp   undergrowth

Activities

Visit: safari park. Local museum may have stuffed animals.
Songs: Cannibal King
         Down in the jungle
Poem: A thousand hairy savages (Spike Milligan)
Story: The mouse and the lion
Drama: different animals
         Tarzan swinging through the trees
         hunter cutting his way through the undergrowth
         walking through a swamp

Art work

Make masks from papier mâché.
Make faces on wood with pasta, e.g. lentils for nose, macaroni for
   eyebrows, assorted pasta shapes for eyes, mouth and hair.
Make brightly coloured necklaces from painted pasta.
Make bongo drums (see Music, page 98).
Make a jungle collage:
   lion (sand and wood shavings)
   monkey (brown fabric)
   crocodile (egg-boxes)
   elephant (newspaper)
   giraffe (prints with paint)
   tree-house (cardboard box, painted)
   mud-hut (brown, crayon with straw roof)
   trees (leaves or leaf prints and brown paint)
   vines (green string, winding in and out)

Animals
(see also Chapter 8: Music and Movement; Zoos)

Points for discussion

Domestic	Woodland and countryside	Wild
cow	badger	elephant
pig	fox	tiger
sheep	squirrel	lion
hen	hedgehog	zebra
dog	snake	giraffe
cat	fieldmouse	kangaroo
horse	bat	monkey
bull	hare	leopard
goat	mole	hippopotamus
donkey	deer	rhinoceros
	lizard	gorilla
Pets	stoat	deer
tortoise	weasel	crocodile
hamster		dolphin
guinea pig		shark
rabbit		sloth
gerbil		bear
mouse		polar bear
		snake
		sea-lion

Comparisons

four-legged	horns	spots
two-legged	smallest	slow
no legs	long necks	trunk
fast	stripes	biggest

Interesting words

neigh	moo	run
snort	roar	trot
snuffle	chatter	charge
miaow	climb	jaws
bark	slither	claws
trumpet	swing	footprints
crow	jump	camouflage
baa		

animal doctor: vet   fictitious: dragon; monsters

Activities

Visits: (see Nature, page 73)
Poems: Ning, Nang, Nong (Spike Milligan)
         Jabberwocky
Song: The elephant goes like this and that
         (see also Music and Movement, pages 110, 111)

Art work

Always make sure the material is suitable for the animal:
    wool, fur fabric or velvet for monkeys, horse;
    egg-boxes for crocodiles, dragons;
    dark plastic, leather strips or torn newspaper for elephants,
       dolphins, rhinos, hippos, sharks;
    sand for lion, tiger, leopard, horse;
    potato prints for giraffe, crocodile, dragon or leopard.

Make a histogram of animals:

Horns	*Grey*	*Stripes*
cow	elephant	badger
deer	dolphin	zebra
goat	hippo	tiger
bull	rhino	some deer

Patches	*Mane*
leopard	horse
cheetah	lion
giraffe	

Make a histogram of animals seen, for example:
    At the Farm: 5 hens, 10 cows, 2 dogs, 1 cat.

Autumn

(see also Nature, page 69)

Points for discussion

Colours	*Shapes*	*Evergreen trees*
red	different leaf	fir
brown	shapes	holly
orange	oak	pine (cones)
yellow	beech	
	horse chestnut	*Fruit*
	maple (large)	conkers
	silver birch	acorns
	(small)	berries
	leaves fall from	
	trees	

Interesting words
(see also Nature, page 69)

harvest	combine	hibernate
farmer	harvester	bulbs
plough	burrs	weather

weather becomes colder
animals start to hibernate (tortoise, squirrel, badger)
some birds fly to warmer countries − migrate
plant bulbs now for early Spring (see Nature, page 64).

Activities
Special events:
  Hallowe'en
  Bonfire Night − warn of dangerous fireworks − sparklers only for child.
Hymn: We plough the fields and scatter
Song: Farmer, farmer, sow your seed
Drama: leaves fluttering from trees
    squirrel scuttling around to collect food
    children collecting wood
    fireworks − shooting up, falling down, spinning, jumping, abruptly stopping
    Hallowe'en − witches on broomsticks, stirring cauldron etc.

Art work
Leaf prints.
Dried and pressed leaves made into pictures. For example, thin man
  made of ferns, fat man made of horse-chestnut leaves.
Bark rubbing.
Necklace made of melon seeds, etc.
Trees of corrugated cardboard with cornflake leaves.
Pine-cone mobiles hung from twigs.
Hallowe'en mobile – black silhouettes of cats, moon, stars, witch,
  cauldron, pointed hats, broomstick.
Make a Guy for Bonfire Night.
Make a scarecrow collage.
Fruit prints.

Birds
(see also Chapter 5: Nature)

Points for discussion

Fly wild	Domestic	Pets
pigeon	swan ... swims	budgie
sparrow	duck ... swims	parrot
blackbird	chicken	minah
thrush	hen	
blue tit	cockerel, rooster	*Zoo*
starling	goose	penguin ... swims also
owl		emu ⎫ do not fly
magpie		ostrich ⎭
chaffinch		peacock
cuckoo		

different noises: squawk, crow, sing, chirp, tweet, twit-twoo,
cluck, cuckoo

Interesting words

swoop	soar	swift
flutter	waddle	sweep
glide	flap	skim
dive	drift	

Story and song: The ugly duckling
                  Four and twenty blackbirds
Drama: gliding swan
                  chicken walk
                  proud peacock
                  waddling penguin
                  pecking the ground

Art work

Birds make lovely mobiles from paper shapes, with curled paper for
    tails and feathers.
Fluffy chickens can be made from yellow cotton-wool balls (for
    Easter, add white paper eggshells).
Penguins and owls make good collages. Use a basic oval shape, with
    two triangular feet, a triangular beak, two large round eyes and a
    pair of wings.
Peacocks also make good collages. They can be angled from the front
    or a side view. The gorgeous tail feathers can be created with blue
    and green hand prints, sequins, tin foil, coloured metallic paper or
    potato prints.
Make a histogram of the birds seen from the classroom window.

Blowing

Points for discussion

(The ESNs child needs to be taught to breathe correctly, and not to be
lazy by only using the top half of his lungs.)

Musical instruments	Items to blow	Wind blows
whistle	party blower	paper
trumpet	balloon	leaves
mouth organ	bubbles	feather
trombone	dandelion clock	washing
flute	foot pump	long hair
bagpipes	balloon pump	clouds
tuba	bicycle pump	kite
recorder	air-bed	windmill
melodica	tyre	yacht
comb and paper	empty aerosol can	
	cardboard tube	
	bellows	
	hairdryer	

Interesting words

breathe	pant	lungs
breath	wheeze	breeze
huff	draught	inhale
puff	air	exhale
gasp		

Activities

Visit: music shop (look in window only, if necessary)
             marina (yachts)
             hairdresser's shop
Story: Three little pigs (huff, puff)
Songs: Puff the magic dragon
             Blowin' in the wind
             A mouse lived in a windmill in old Amsterdam
Movement: floating down (paper, feather)
             floating up (balloon, bubbles, kite)
             windmill sails spinning
             inflated air-bed (puffed out, lightweight)

Art work

Blow painting (see Creative activities, page 23).

Blow up a balloon – paint it.

Blow bubbles; paint the bubbles seen – lots of circles in different colours and sizes.

Make a collage of blowing musical instruments, using metallic paper.

Make a picture of a windy day (this could be used for the weather chart too!): washing on line; leaves blowing from the tree; umbrella blown inside out; hat blown off; kite in sky.

Make a kite – fly it in a nearby park.

Make small windmills on sticks, to blow.

Make model windmills out of yoghurt cartons and lollipop sticks.

Blow dandelion clock over painted sticky surface.

Blow flower petals over sticky surface.

Make a picture of a fat bandsman blowing a trumpet.

Body parts
(See also Faces)

Points for discussion

hands, feet	chin, cheek,	calf
elbows, knees,	forehead	thigh
ankles	blood	ear lobe
neck, shoulders	bones	scar
head	muscles	skeleton
legs, arms	fingernails	adam's apple
fingers, toes	toenails	thumbs
boy, girl	knuckles	heel
back, front, side	shin	

different body parts for animals, fish, and birds

Interesting words
profile   tissue

Activities
Visit: local museum for skeletons
Songs: Head and shoulders, knees and toes
        One finger, one thumb, keep moving
        Dem bones, dem bones, dem dry bones
Drama: genii (all body and arms, magic)
        robot (mechanical, stiff)
        dalek (gliding, no arms or legs)
        spaceman (weightless, floating)
        diver (plunging down)
        animals, birds and fish

Art work
Hand prints (not black paint!).
Foot prints – walking up wall, along ceiling.
One single giant's hand/foot filled with each child's hand or foot
   print.
Magazine pictures of shoes, hands, gloves, feet.
Boy/girl contrast in clothes: life size, draw around tallest child lying
   down. This is ——— (label on body parts).
Draw round hand and cut out.

Hand prints – display ideas:
  yellow, orange, red formed in a circle to make a sun;
  hand prints formed into a flower, paint the stalk, one
  single hand print serves as leaf;
  crayon over card, from which hand shape (template of hand) has
  been cut.
Large eye, made from magazine eyes, black circle in centre, black
  curled paper around edge to represent lashes – looks like a giant
  spider!
Funny people, collages of mixed-up men, women, children, for
  example baby's face on man's body wearing high heels, etc. Cut
  from magazines, catalogues. Also mixed-up animals, birds, fish.
  Could be game for class.
Make vegetable people, using potatoes, carrots, grapes (good for eyes),
  dried apricots for feet and cocktail sticks joining them together.

Buildings
(see also Homes)

Points for discussion

skyscraper	greenhouse	hospital
church	tower	office block
school	castle	library
shop	windmill	bungalow
lighthouse	hotel	college
igloo	factory	university
thatched cottage	mill	theatre
supermarket	palace	mud hut
hypermarket	flat	town hall
market garden	house	

Special buildings:

Eiffel Tower	Buckingham	Big Ben
Blackpool Tower	Palace	Windsor Castle
	Leaning Tower (Pisa)	

Materials: bricks, wood, glass, mortar.

Interesting words

construction	timber	foundations	brickie

Activities

Visit: building sites
church
factory, if possible
supermarket
lighthouse, if possible
} contrast shape, size, noise (echoes)

Songs: Tall shops in the town
A mouse lived in a windmill in old Amsterdam

Story: Three little pigs

Art work

Make a skyline collage, all shapes and sizes of skyscrapers and a church seen in silhouette at night.

Make Blackpool scene – crisscross black string or shoelaces for tower, with people sunbathing on beach in front.

Make a series of contrasting buildings:
greenhouse (tin foil or cling film)
thatched cottage (sand, with raffia roof)
windmill (hand prints)
igloo (square, white potato prints on black paper).

Paint assorted cardboard boxes for buildings, stick on squares of coloured paper for windows and doors. Build skyscraper flats with matchboxes. Make a fairytale castle or space station with tubes, cones and yoghurt pots. Spray gold or silver – don't spray polystyrene, it will melt.

Charts

Kind to make

weather (see Weather, page 226)
girls
boys
} – numbers in class and names
picture timetable
days of week
date of month
} in regular use, but more interesting to child if he has helped to make them

(referring to children in class, and usually only the older classes)

What pets have you at home?

What colour are your eyes?

Who wears tights, long or short socks?

What do you like most? ⎱ food, TV, in school, pop star, football
What do you like least? ⎰ team

What did you see at the ——— ? (place of visit)

What does a butcher sell? ⎫
What does the Post Office sell? ⎬ good for contrasts and comparisons
What does the greengrocer sell? ⎭

How many brothers/sisters have you?

What is your favourite colour?

Chinese

Points for discussion

dragons	lion	kite
Chinaman	Pekenese dog	kimono
lantern	Kung Fu	chopsticks
coolie	paddy-fields	chop-suey
pagoda	rice	yellow
parasol		

Interesting words

sampan (water vehicle)

rickshaw (land vehicle, man powered)

Chinese lanterns are of interest – they are from a dried plant with pretty orange lantern shapes.

Activities

Song: Puff the magic dragon

Drama: shuffling

pulling a rickshaw (describe it as being like a wheelbarrow, going the other way)

Story: Aladdin and his lamp

Art work
Use very bright colours, lots of braid and sequins.

Make a dragon, with coloured felt, braid, bright buttons, sequins; include claws or fiery breath; can be upright or horizontal (like a lizard). Green hand prints, egg-boxes or vegetable prints, can be fierce or cartoon-like.

Contrast shapes:
pagoda – made of tiered boxes, painted and decorated;
kite – crossed sticks and paper;
round parasol – decorate broken umbrella;
make lanterns, with black paper and coloured cellophane.

Make a kite and fly it.

Make a paper boat with tissue paper, sail fixed with cocktail stick.

Christmas

Points for discussion

story of Jesus	star of	gifts
born in stable	Bethlehem	Father Christmas
three kings	Mary	presents
shepherds	Joseph	reindeer
angels	animals	robins

Activities
(see also Chapter 7: Music)
Carols: Away in a manger
          We three kings
Songs: Rudolf, the red-nosed reindeer
          Little drummer boy
          I saw three ships
Drama: act the Nativity
          mime any other Bible story
          Father Christmas, making and delivering presents
          Christmas morning, child opening presents

Art work
(a)   Religious:
      Make a Nativity scene, 3-D in cardboard box for stable, suspending a star above box. Black silhouetted figures against a pale blue background. Figures to be included: Mary and Joseph, Baby Jesus, Three Kings/Wise Men, Shepherds, Angel.

Universal figure
(change head-dress for King)

Simple angel

Easy stars to copy

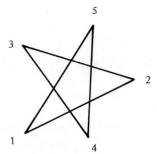

(b) Traditional:
Father Christmas, reindeer, sledge, robin, Christmas cake, Yule
log, holly, plum pudding, turkey, Christmas trees, snow,
snowman, snowflakes, presents, decorations, paper-chains,
paper hats, lanterns, candles, carol singers, bells, stockings,
sacks.

Clothes

Points for discussion

Man	Both	Lady
shirt	gloves	blouse
tie	scarf	skirt
trousers	jeans	frock
socks	T-shirt	dress
swimming trunks	coat	tights
jacket	underwear	swimsuit
waistcoat	shoes	bikini
	boots	
	sandals	
	jumper	
	hat	

Children	Babies
wellington boots	nappies
vests	sleeping suits
bonnet	

Interesting words

turban	fez	kimono
clogs	yashmak	balaclava
kilt	sari	draper
poncho		

Activities

Visits: clothes shops – men's and women's
            tailor's
            launderette
            shoe shop

Movement: washing wafting on line in breeze
            mime getting dressed up

Game: Who am I describing? (She's wearing a red dress,
            brown sandals, etc.)

Song: Soldier, soldier, will you marry me?

Art work

Picture collage of washing on line.
Collage of assorted clothes cut from magazines.
Collage of assorted footwear cut from magazines (shoes, sandals, boots
    etc.)

Make a scarecrow – turnip for head (or balloon), stuffed sack for body, sticks for arms and legs. Dress him and paint face. *Or* small carton for head, larger for body, empty tin-foil tubes for arms and legs. Dress him and paint face.

Dress a simple peg doll.

Make a Guy for Bonfire Night out of old stockings (legs) and socks (arms), an old pillowslip for his body and a deflated ball for his head; stuff the stockings, socks and pillowslip with old newspaper tightly screwed up. Dress him up in *very* old clothes.

Colour

Points for discussion

Good contrasts	Primary	Secondary
black and white	red	green
yellow and blue	blue	orange
blue and white	yellow	purple
yellow and black		turquoise
brown and yellow		grey
blue and green		pink
red and black		mauve
green and white		
red, white and blue		

Colour is involved in everything:

traffic-lights	TV	nature
clothes	flags	food
make-up		

Colour blindness usually involves red/green confusion.

Interesting words

rainbow	sparkling	vivid
dull	shiny	dark
bright		

Activities

Songs: I am mixing colours
          I can sing a rainbow

Provide a colour table to show variation in one colour.

Art work

All art work is colourful!

Make colour charts.

Make series of simple flags:

(a) The Union Jack is made up of three flags altogether:
     white background with a broad red cross (St George)
     white diagonals on a blue background (St Andrew)
     red diagonals on a white background (St Patrick).

(b) Other (more simple) flags are:
     a broad red cross on a white background (Switzerland)
     a red circle in the centre of a white flag (Japan)
     white stars on a blue background in the top corner and broad red
     and white stripes (USA)
     one crescent moon and one star, both white on a red background
     (Turkey).

Faces
(see also Body parts; People)

Points for discussion

Mood	*People*	*Animals*
happy	clown	elephant (long nose)
sad	monster	deer, cow (horns)
winking	vampire	pig (snout)
blinking	robot	cat (whiskers)
angelic	baby	rabbit (whiskers)
evil	lady	sheep
angry	man	dog
tearful	child	fish (one eye only
excited	old person	seen at once)
sleepy	pop star	birds (no mouth, no
giggly	witch	ears, only beak)
weary	wizard	
	Old Father Time	
	Red Indian	

Features	Hair	Additions
eyes	curly	glasses
nose	long	sunglasses
mouth	short	make-up
nostrils	straight	goggles
chin	bald	masks
cheeks	fair	beard
lips	dark	moustache
teeth	red	visor
ears	grey	veil
temple	white	sideboards
forehead	plaited	whiskers
eyebrows	bun	
eyelashes	ponytail	
eyelids	crew-cut	
	hairstyle	

Interesting words

wrinkles (laughter-lines, worry-lines)   dimples   pimples

Activities

Songs: My eyes are dim, I cannot see
         Michael Finnigan
Music: make parts of face move to favourite tune (i.e. eyebrows,
         jaw, teeth, eyelids)
Visit: hairdresser's – look in mirrors
Watch teacher putting on make-up.

Art work

Make collage of (a) magazine faces; (b) face parts – cut out and pasted
    overlapping each other.
Paint clown's face on a carton; throw air-flow balls or bean bags into
    wide-open mouth.
Cut faces out of large turnips, swedes, etc., especially at Hallowe'en.
Make masks out of cardboard plates. Paint and decorate with 'war-
    paint' for Indian warriors.
Cut out eyes, nose, mouth from tin-foil plate, stick coloured
    cellophane over the holes, hang in front of window.
Make mobile face out of card; cut out a hat, eyes, nose, moustache,
    mouth, bow-tie and string them fairly close together. Paint both
    sides of the card.

Choose fairly large polished wood shapes – glue pasta shapes on wood for features, use wood shavings for hair.

Make collage of silhouetted faces out of black paper, e.g. witch, robot, Red Indian (with peace pipe), baby (with dummy), old man (with beard), monster (like Frankenstein, with high forehead).

Make animal-face collage – include elephant, giraffe, zebra, hippopotamus, fish (only one eye), birds (to show only eyes and beak).

Shaped face – make simple pictures of faces inside squares, triangles, etc.

Farms
(see also Animals)

Points for discussion

Animals	Young	Home
horse	foal	stable
cow	calf	cowshed
pig	piglet	sty
hen	chicken	coop
dog	puppy	kennel
cat	kitten	
duck	duckling	
sheep	lamb	
cockerel or rooster		
farmer	tractor	

Interesting words

shepherd	milkmaid	incubator
foodstuff	machinery	combine harvester
plough	vet	battery chickens

Activities

Visit:	farm, agricultural show
Song:	Old Macdonald had a farm
Drama:	mime – farmer's work, sowing seeds, cutting corn, milking cows, shearing sheep
Movement:	seeds growing
	various farm animals

Art work

An actual 3-D model of a farm is very hard for the ESNs child to make, unless there are some small plastic animals in class. The teacher could make some matching pictures of animals, their young and their homes for the class to play with as a table game.

Make a 'tractor' to play in, out of large cardboard boxes.

Animals are easier to draw if the picture shows them lying down; cotton-wool will do for sheep.

A cockerel makes a superb collage with very bright colours, sequins, gay material or hand prints with red felt for the crown.

Festivals

St Valentine's Day (14 February)
Celebrated between sweethearts (for teenagers only): send cards to boyfriend/girlfriend/favourite teacher or Mum and Dad. Red heart-shaped cards most suitable – push a cardboard arrow through the heart.

Easter (variable date)
Religious story. Death and resurrection of Jesus. Celebration of rebirth, therefore notice many cards of young animals, e.g. bunnies, chickens, lambs, eggs. Also chocolate Easter Eggs. Make Easter cards out of animal shape or broken eggshell shape. Paint and decorate hard-boiled eggs – brown ones make better faces. Shell can be dyed by boiling in water with food colouring added.

Mother's Day (variable date)
Make Mother's Day cards. Make paper flowers as gift, or pot-pourri (combined herbs and rose petals, very dry, in pretty container), or simple pomander – orange studded with cloves and tied with broad ribbon. Seniors should practise doing Mother's Day work in class and be taught to help Mother as much as possible on her day of rest.

Father's Day (variable date)
Make Father's Day cards. Suitable gifts: shell-covered trinket box (for cuff links); fringed bookmarker with fancy stitching, or model made during handicrafts session. Older children should be taught to help Dad, e.g. clean his car on his day of rest.

Harvest (variable date)
Thanksgiving ceremony for providing food. Collect harvest food, fruit and vegetables and, after Assembly, sort it out for child to take to nearby Old People's Home or other needy cause. Not everyone is as lucky as he is for food. Farmer sows oats, wheat, barley to make bread and cereals. Make a scarecrow in class.

Hallowe'en (31 October)
Night of goblins and witches, spooky, eerie, frightening. Make hats, masks; pictures of witches, cauldrons, broomsticks, cats, stars, moon. Good for drama and movement activities.

Bonfire Night (5 November)
Warn of dangerous fireworks. Make a Guy. Fireworks in music and movement. Bonfire Night collage, made up of old *used* fireworks. Food, treacle toffee, parkin and baked potatoes.

Cards for special occasions
(a) Silhouette with spattered background

(b) Cut-out shape

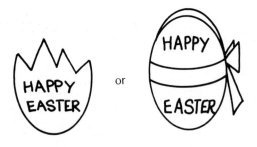

(c) Collage, screwed-up tissue-paper

Mother's Day card

Father's Day card

(d) Pop-up card

Fold paper in half twice to make the card shape (Figure 1). Open up the card and fold the inside crease in the opposite direction. Cut horizontally through the crease (Figure 2). Fold back the edges to make two triangles (Figure 3), then fold the triangles over the other way and back again to make the folds workable. Open up the card and manipulate the pop-up part until it pops up correctly when the card is opened (Figure 4).

A typical design to draw around the pop-up card is shown in Figure 5.

More suggestions for pop-up cards: other birds; fish; a whale.

Figure 1   Figure 2   Figure 3

Figure 4   Figure 5

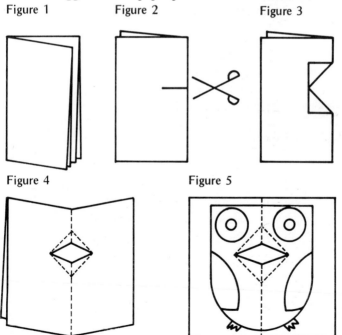

Fish

Points for discussion

Fish for eating	*Assorted sizes*	*Other fish*
cod	long, thin	goldfish
haddock	flat	shark
kipper	fat	angel-fish
plaice	many fins	sword fish
hake	few fins	eel
trout		

All fish swim and live in water *all the time*.

Interesting words

   underwater   scales   aquarium   gills

Activities

Visits:	go fishing in nearby pond
	look at aquaria in pet shops
	goldfish in garden centre pond
	zoos and safari parks, aquaria
	fishmonger's shop
	fish market
	fishing town, village, docks
Songs:	One, two, three, four, five
	(Once I caught a fish alive)
	All the fish are swimming in the water
Movement:	wriggling fish
	squirming when caught
	swimming

Art work

Make a collage of graded fish: huge one with mouth open, eating smaller one with mouth open, eating smaller one, etc.

Making a classroom pond: strong polythene lining a large wooden box; put pebbles and some stones in the bottom. Fill with pond water and keep *a few* tadpoles or some terrapins.

When making fish use circles of cellophane or other suitable material to represent the scales.

Make fishing 'nets' (of jam-jars and string) to go fishing in a nearby pond.

Flowers
(see also Chapter 5: Nature; Autumn)

Points for discussion
colours	real flowers	smells (scented)
gardens	plastic flowers	long leaves
bees (honey)	dried flowers	round leaves
shapes	paper flowers	prickly leaves
butterflies	prickly thorns	

Bright colours are to attract insects and birds.

Interesting words
   pollen   bud   petal   stem

Common flowers
snowdrop	tulip	dandelion
rose	daisy	poppy
daffodil	clover	

Activities
Visit: parks and gardens in Spring
              garden centres
              florist's shop
              wild flowers in fields and woods
Song: Where have all the flowers gone?
Movement: waving like flowers in breeze
              nodding heads
              growing from a tiny seed

Art work
(see also Paper flowers, page 37)
Flowers can be made of almost anything – cloth, paper, mosaic, pasta, hand prints or foot prints. Make 3-D daffodils from an egg-box painted yellow, and glue a single segment to the centre of fringed yellow paper.
Massed flowers make an attractive collage. They can be painted or cut from wallpaper, material, magazines.
Flowers can be displayed singly to frame a picture or grouped together in a vase.
For ways of preserving natural flowers, see Nature, page 70.

Flying
(see also Transport; Insects; Birds)

Points for discussion

Machines	Fictional	Using wind
aeroplane	magic carpet	kite
helicopter	flying saucer	glider
jet	witch	hang-gliding
balloon		parachute
rocket		insects
airship		birds
sea-plane		bats
wind	sky	clouds
air	atmosphere	wings

Interesting words

propellers	dive	take-off
engines	swoop	touch down
Zeppelin	loop-the-loop	taxi
hangar	hover	

Activities

Visits: airport
gliding school, if possible
birds in zoo or park
take kite to park

Songs: Those magnificent men in their flying machines
That daring young man on the flying trapeze
Blowin' in the wind

Movement: fly like a jet plane
hover like a bird
float like clouds
float down like a parachute

Art work

Make a kite, fly it in the park.

Anything which flies is useful for a mobile.

Make a 3-D balloon with crisscrossed string or cotton, joining a basket underneath.

Make a space station with tubes, cones, yoghurt pots and tin foil — suspend flying saucer (two paper plates, decorated) above station.

Fruit
(see also Chapter 5: Nature; Chapter 4: Cookery)

Points for discussion

Sweet	*Sour*	*Dried*
eating apple	lemon	sultana
tangerine	grapefruit	currant
pineapple	lime	raisin
melon	some grapes	date
cherries		fig
grapes		prune
peach		
banana		
tomato		

Tart (needs cooking)	*Soft*	*Unusual fruit*
baking apple	blackcurrant	pomegranate
rhubarb	whinberry	avocado pear
plum	bilberry	guava
damson	strawberry	lichee
apricot	blackberry	mango
	raspberry	

Fruit with stones, with pips, with tiny seeds. Eat it with peel, without peel, cook it first. Soft, brown part (bruising) nasty taste. Look at size and shape. When shopping, do you buy one or a pound (in weight) or a punnet?

Activities
Visit: market
        market garden
        orchard in season
        greengrocer's
        supermarket
        hypermarket
Song: Oranges and lemons

Art work

Large magazine pictures of fruit are excellent for collages.

Pineapple has an interesting skin, good to represent by printing; make leaves from green crêpe paper.

Make fruit prints.

Make fruit mosaics, i.e. tiny pieces of paper cut up inside giant fruit.

Dried out (flat) orange, grapefruit, lemon and lime peel look effective when cut into neat segments and arranged into pictures, e.g. flowers.

Furniture

Points for discussion

chair	drawers	plain
rocking chair	bookcase	shiny
armchair	cupboard	wooden
table	suite	metal
desk	cabinet	plastic
coffee table	soft	cloth
cot	hard	glass
bed	ornaments	picture
sofa	patterned	lights up
settee		

Furniture for lying on; sitting on; eating from. Just for decoration, or for use?

Interesting words

antique	polished	display

Activities

Look at classroom furniture and school furniture – not apparatus.

Visit: furniture shop

Story: Goldilocks and the three bears

Drama: mime using furniture, as in story

Art work

Divide large paper into four compartments labelled bedroom, bathroom, living room, kitchen. Place pictures of appropriate furniture in each compartment.

Make pretend furniture from cardboard boxes.

Make dolls' furniture in woodwork.

Glass
(not advisable with younger class)

Points for discussion

window, shapes of windows
door
TV screen
light bulb
bottles – assorted shapes
jam-jars
other containers e.g. coffee jars
car windows, windscreen

mirror, shapes of mirrors
fish tank
clock face
spectacles
glasses
greenhouses (purpose: all
glass, lets in sun and light)
stained-glass windows
glass around swimming pool

Glass is *transparent*, so *we can see through it*. Bottles and jars easy to see when empty. Bathroom and toilet windows are different, for privacy.

Interesting words

transparent   opaque   visor   goggles

Activities

Visits: church with stained-glass windows
           greenhouses
Song: My eyes are dim, I cannot see

Art work

Make a stained-glass-window effect, by cutting out holes from black paper and placing coloured cellophane behind holes. Hang picture in front of window to get full stained-glass effect.

Make peep-boxes to see through, using clear cellophane, not glass. Place small model dolls or plastic animals standing in *Plasticine* in a painted scene. Cover with cellophane. Can be made so child peeps through the top or in the side. A nativity scene is particularly attractive.

Teacher could paint pictures on classroom windows for child's pleasure.

Hats

Points for discussion

sombrero	jockey's cap	fireman's helmet
bowler	busby	top-hat
trilby	hood	bonnet
cap	helmet	beret
stetson	crash helmet	feathered head-dress
headscarf	policeman's	mantilla
turban	helmet	fez

Contrasting shapes

round bowler	oval busby	triangular headscarf
square top-hat	flat cap	

Some are for *identification* and some for *protection*.

Activities

Song: In my Easter Bonnet

Drama: Guess who's wearing what hat by his movements, for example motorcyclist, jockey, guardsman.

Art work

Make Easter Bonnets – have a best-hat parade around the school.

Make a collage of assorted hats.

The teacher could make a game for the class: Which hat belongs to which body (e.g. policeman, nurse, guardsman, cowboy, Indian).

Homes
(see also Buildings)

Points for discussion

Building	Inhabitant	Other homes
igloo	Eskimo	thatched cottage
caravan	gipsy	house
castle	King/Queen	bungalow
teepee (wigwam)	Indian	flat
farmhouse	farmer	terraced
tent	camper	semi-detached
lighthouse	lighthouse-keeper	detached
windmill	miller	town house

Think about:
(a)   shapes: round igloo, lighthouse, windmill; square house; triangular wigwam, tent
(b)   different rooms: upstairs; downstairs (cellar, attic, loft, spiral staircase).
       Use *Lego* bricks for demonstrating.

Activities
Visits: building site
           lighthouse, if possible
           windmill, if possible
           teacher's house or flat
Song: A mouse lived in a windmill in old Amsterdam
           The windmill sails go round and around

Art work
A fairytale castle can be made from cartons, tubes and yoghurt pots with lots of tin foil and bright paint.
The child could draw his own home.
The teacher could draw child's home from his description; child colours it in.
The Wendy House in the classroom could be decorated with pictures done by the class.
A gypsy caravan makes a very gay collage, with lots of braid and bright colours.
Igloos are fine made from potato prints – white on black paper.
Child can build skyscraper flats of his own out of matchboxes, suitably painted.
Older child can build with playing cards – needs patience and good balance.

Insects
(see also Flying)

Points for discussion

Flying	*Crawling*	
fly	beetle	spider (not
bee	ant	strictly an
wasp	centipede	insect, but
dragonfly	caterpillar	cannot be
butterfly	wood-louse	explained to
ladybird	grub	an ESNs child)
daddy-long-legs	worm	
moth	chrysalis	
bluebottle	spider's web	

Interesting words

crawl	sting	pounce (spider)
flutter	swarm	buzz
scuttle	wriggle	

Activities

Visits: local park – turn up stones
                  school grounds – digging up soil
                  keep a wormery

Songs/poems: There's a worm at the bottom of the garden
                  Incy wincy spider
                  Little Arabella Millar
                  Little Miss Muffet

Movement: busy as a bee
                  fluttery butterfly
                  creepy spider suddenly pounces
                  wriggly caterpillar
                  busy ants

Art work

Insects make attractive mobiles – their wings could be made from folded tissue-paper circles.

Bees in and around the hive make a colourful collage. Choose bright yellow and orange materials.

Ladybirds could be painted black or red, with the opposite coloured sticky paper used to represent spots.

Make a spider from blackened pipe cleaners; make its web from strong cotton or nylon thread.

Jobs
(see also Hats)

Points for discussion

miner	fireman	milkman
policeman	farmer	train driver
nurse	fisherman	dustbinman
doctor	postman	builder
dentist	baker	vet
porter	conductor	clown
shopkeeper	chimney-sweep	teacher
bus driver		

The *Ladybird* books are an excellent source of people's jobs.
Some jobs require uniforms for protection or identification.

Activities

Visits:	fire station
	bus depot (ride on buses)
	railway station
	farm
	shops
Visitors:	may be willing to come to school on request, and even bring films to show children: for example, policeman, fireman, dentist
Poems/songs:	The dustbinman
	The farmer's in his den
	Pat-a-cake, pat-a-cake, baker's man
	Rub-a-dub-dub
Movement:	guess who child is by walk or mime

Art work

Make a chart of people: those we know, those we visited and those who visited us.

Follow-up work of all visits.

Silhouette suggestion: make large double-decker bus — place a silhouette in each window, for example: milkman (peaked cap and milk bottle); chimney-sweep (flat cap and sweep's brush); policeman (helmet); fireman (helmet and axe); miner (helmet and light with shovel); postman (peaked cap and letters); bus driver (at front); conductor (at rear); baby (with dummy in his mouth).

Leaves
(see also Chapter 5: Nature; Autumn)

Points for discussion

Shape
long and narrow (spider plant,
   grass)
rounded (oak)
palmate (five-fingered) (horse
   chestnut)

Feel or texture
furry (geranium, petunia)
prickly (sea holly, holly, gorse)

Appearance
shiny (holly, rhododendron)
striped (spider plant)
spotted (laurel, ivy)
edible (cabbage, lettuce)
scented (herbs, e.g. mint and
   geraniums)

Some leaves fall from trees in Winter. Those that don't are
protected from snow by having a thick, shiny or spiny appearance.
Preserve in glycerine – see page 70.

Interesting words

forest   shrub   bush
evergreen   jungle   foliage
branch   twig

Activities

Visit: a forest
              a nature trail
              parks and gardens
              (collect leaves on visit)
Song: Five little leaves so bright and gay
Movement: waving in breeze
              kicking up leaves
              twisting and wafting down to ground
              blown along ground at intervals

Art work

Make pictures and designs with dried leaves: for example, make a
   man with fern leaves for his arms and legs, a horse-chestnut leaf
   for his body and a geranium leaf for his head.
Make leaf prints.
Collect many coloured leaves and make a collage – glue them inside
   giant leaf shape.
Grade the leaves collected, using smallest leaf first up to biggest leaf.
   Display in a line.

Metal

Points for discussion

Metal names

copper
gold
brass
tin
silver
iron
steel

Machinery
(see also Transport)

car
bicycle
aeroplane
robot
Dalek
tractor

School or household items

clock	tins	*Other metal items*
knife, fork, spoon	waste-bin	spear
button	buckle	shield
jewellery	milk-bottle tops	horseshoe
saucepans	new pence	nails
tin foil	trumpet	screws
gate	some tables/	stainless steel
scissors	chairs	dustbin
	kettle	hammer

Interesting words

cutlery	shiny	glittery
coins	gilt	gilded
metallic	wrought-ironwork	

Activities

Visit: hardware store
kitchenware department in large store
blacksmith (if possible)

Songs: My grandfather's clock
Half a sixpence
I have a sixpence
Peter plays with one hammer

Movement: move like the hands of a clock, slowly
robot, Dalek
move in pairs, jerkily, backwards and forwards like a
machine

Polish coins and old metal with *Duraglit* or *Silver Dip*.
Ask local brass band to play in school.

Art work
(Always use very strong paper for metal collages.)
Make a metal collage – bits and pieces glued in abstract pattern.
Make a metal collage of an object, for example a tractor or aeroplane.
Make a picture of an untidy dustbin showing all metal contents.
Make a clock face with small metal buttons.
Make a collage of circles using money, bottle-tops, curtain rings, metal buttons, cogs and wheels from toys.

Number
(see also Charts)

Points for discussion and Activities
1   One-to-one correspondence: one straw per milk bottle; one spoon per cup; one egg per egg-cup, etc.
2   Matching like for like: shapes; colours; pictures.
3   Sorting: hot/cold   heavy/light
             hollow/solid   small/big
             sharp/blunt   open/closed
             dark/light   thick/thin
4   Weighing, measuring, balancing: many table games are available for the older child.
5   Amounts of money are useful to learn.
6   Some add-and-subtract games for the older child to play.
7   The older child can measure classroom objects; for example, he may find that one table is eight matchboxes (or straws, etc.) long, while another is ten matchboxes long. Therefore 'this table *is shorter than* that'.

    More examples of comparison: longer than; the same as; wider than; taller than, more, less, thicker than, hotter than.

Songs: Five currant buns
         Five little ducks
         One, two, three, four, five
         Ten green bottles
         Five little speckled frogs, etc.

Art work
(see also Charts for ideas where children can illustrate number graphically)
To illustrate numbers in the classroom, the teacher must make both the written figure and the number in the same colour and material.

Another idea for a chart is to make a picture of an octopus, a man, a bird, a ladybird and a fish. Underneath, or at the side of, each animal should be the number of legs. The older child could be encouraged to observe which animal has the most number of legs and which has the least number.

Outer space

Points for discussion

rockets	planets	lunar
spacemen	robot	flying saucer
moon	stars	space-ship
moon buggy	weightlessness	splashdown
parachute	Apollo	shooting stars
Martians	Jupiter	America
Mars	Pluto	Russia
Venus		

Interesting words

lunar module	meteors	cosmonauts
space module	comets	astronauts
link-up	telescope	

Activities

Visit: observatory, e.g. Jodrell Bank (if possible)
Song: Twinkle, twinkle, little star
Hey-diddle-diddle
Story: Dan Dare, Dr Who, Star Trek, Star Wars
Movement/Drama: weightlessness
shooting stars (down); rocket (up)
child explores unknown planet
child imagines he is a Martian

Art work

Man from outer space made from boxes covered with tin foil; single egg compartments for eyes and nose, pipe-cleaner feelers, etc.
Imaginary art for child to paint:
on the moon
space plants
men from outer space
a new planet.

Make a space station with plastic containers, boxes and tubes set in *Polyfilla* and screwed-up newspaper.

Make a lunarscape with weird shapes of bent wire, pipe cleaners, scraps of polystyrene and other waste materials set in *Polyfilla*.

Make an abstract design with screws, nuts, bolts, bottle tops, etc. Again, it could be set in *Polyfilla*.

Paper

Points for discussion

tissue	crêpe	wrapping paper
card	streamers	paper carrier-bag
magazine	decorations	cardboard carton
some games	corrugated paper	book
newspaper	wallpaper	envelope
comic	paper cup	letter

Paper comes from trees.

Interesting words
  packaging

Activities
Poem: If all the world was paper
Song: Paperback writer
Movement/Drama: fluttering down like tissue-paper
                    playing in a carton
                    opening a letter
                    reading a comic

Art work

Make a collage of assorted papers, all brightly coloured, various thicknesses.

Make a picture, using real, brightly-coloured paper carrier-bag glued on to white paper. Glue assorted papers as if coming out of a bag. If necessary the bag could be stuffed with newspaper and some kinds of paper could be fastened inside the outer edge of the bag to achieve full 3-D effect.

Make paper flowers.

Make paper animals.

Make paper chain at Christmas.

Make display of empty paper food-cartons.

People
(see also Jobs; Faces)

Points for discussion

baby	tall	glasses
man, men	short	beard
boy	fat	long hair
child, children	thin	short hair
lady	bald	mother
woman, women	uncle	father
girl	aunt	brother
nephew	granny, nana	sister
niece	grandad	cousin

Nationality

British	English	Scottish
Irish	Welsh	

Interesting words

foreigner	male	female
race	masculine	feminine
nationality	statue	

Activities

Action rhymes:	Mr Hall is very tall
	Little Arabella Miller
Songs:	Lily the pink
	O, the Grand old Duke of York
	Lucy Locket
	I'm Henry the Eighth, I am, I am
	Michael Finnigan
Visitors:	Many people may be willing to visit the school. Perhaps a blind person could come with his dog.
Movement/drama:	like a fat man
	like a baby
	like a clown
	like a model

Art work

Make a fat, jolly bandsman blowing a bugle.
Make a collage of people cut out from magazines.

Make funny, mixed-up people, for example a baby's face on a man's
body, wearing skirt and bootees! Could be 3-D, with tubes for
body, ping-pong-ball head, crêpe-paper fringed skirt.
Make a robot or spaceman out of cartons covered with tin foil; or
collage of nuts, bolts, screws, wire, shiny buttons, curtain rings,
etc.

Plastic

Points for discussion

some chair covers	pen, biro	plant pots
shoes	litter-bin	plant-pot holders
plastic teaspoons	bucket	cotton-reels
cups, bags	plastic dustbin	some clothing
balls	containers, e.g.	tablecloths
light switch	washing-up	car seats
socket	liquid	milk bottles
plug	egg cartons	food cartons
	many toys	

Plastic is man made (compared with wood, which is natural).

Interesting words

squashy	soft	hard
brittle	bendy	snap
vinyl	PVC	mould
supple	pliable	

Activities
Visit: hardware store: what's metal, what's plastic?
Movement: Contrasts – hard and stiff with soft and bendy.
           Be a bendy toy!

Art work
As before with paper bag and contents. Use plastic bag and display
various plastic containers coming out of bag.
Make display of (empty) plastic food cartons. Compare with display of
paper cartons or (empty) plastic household containers other than
those used for food.
Make collage of plastic substances, stuck on with PVA glue.

Red Indian

Interesting words

Running Bear   Sioux   Cheyenne
Black Foot   Cherokee

Activities

Songs: Ten little Indian boys
     We are the red men
Poem: Hiawatha (Longfellow)
Movement/drama: war dance; rain dance
     Indians stalking food (deer)
     making smoke-signals
     medicine man
     fighting soldiers and cowboys
     riding horses

Art work

Make a 3-D totem pole with different-sized boxes brightly painted and decorated.

A flat picture totem pole is more interesting with a bird, for example an eagle, at the top.

Wigwams can be colourfully made from any bright scraps of material – the background is usually yellow with red, green or brown patterns. There are few circles, nearly all straight line patterns.

Make an Indian head-dress. Make feathers (fringed paper) and secure to long braid for Chief. The warriors only need one or two feathers in a paper band.

Make papier-mâché masks.

Paint pictures of Indians with war-paint.

Shadows and light

Points for discussion

sun	water	moon
lights	shiny surface	ghosts
torch	sun clock	silhouettes
mirror	candle	darkness and light
trees in sun		

shadows caused by light

Interesting words

reflection	spooky	spectre
illumination	eerie	ghoul

Activities

Visit: caves, if possible (e.g. Blue John Mines, Derbyshire; Wookey Hole in Cheddar Gorge)

Movement/drama: jumping over shadows
chasing each other's shadows
making shadows with body/hands
doing what partner does, i.e. being his shadow

Art work

Make shadow objects, e.g. knock many nails into block of wood different sizes and different angles – observe shadows. Child could possibly draw what he sees.

Glue assorted cartons (flat round cheese-cartons, bobbins, tall bottles and square packets) on to a piece of card – observe the shadows.

Almost cut out a shape of sugar-paper, leaving a hinge. Bend it back to observe shadows.

Make own sun clock.

Make picture of a child or man in profile. Cut out the picture on black paper and cut around the picture again. Display both pictures, the black representing the shadow of the main picture.

Shape

Points for discussion

Round	Square	Triangular
ball	some tables	sail of yacht
clock face	chair	headscarf
plate	TV screen	some leaves (ivy)
cup	book	wigwam
record	fireplace	pennant
balloon	bricks	*Other shapes*
wheel	flag	diamond
bubbles		oblong
some tables		oval
		heart-shaped
		star-shaped

Shapes into holes: e.g. drawers into spaces; plug into drain; nest of tables.

The older child could learn how to use a compass to create patterns and round shapes.

Interesting words
    sphere   cube

Activities

Visits: different buildings
                lighthouse or windmill (if possible)
                swimming pool

Songs: Twinkle, twinkle, little star
                The wheels on the bus go round
                Ring-a-ring o' roses

Movements: Make shapes with body, e.g. round and curled up;
                triangle – lying on back, legs and arms joined in air.
                Roll like a ball.
                Float like a bubble.

Art work
(see also Shapes, page 36ff)
Make pictures of graded shapes inside each other.
Make picture of fish blowing bubbles – grade the bubbles.
Build skyscrapers out of square boxes.
Build different-shaped homes, e.g. igloo.

Shops

Points for discussion
Compare the goods sold in different shops.

Grocer	*Greengrocer*	*Butcher*
tinned fruit	fresh vegetables	sausages
tinned vegetables	potatoes	chops
frozen vegetables	cabbage	steak
bread	cauliflower	chicken
cakes	tomatoes	meat
biscuits	carrots	
flour	mushrooms	*Newsagent*
butter	fresh fruit	newspapers
sugar	(apples, pears,	comics
margarine	oranges,	envelopes
cereals	bananas, etc.)	pens
soap		birthday cards
eggs		wrapping paper

Supermarkets sell all of the above items in one large shop.
Other shops and their items could include the chemist, jeweller, baker, furniture shop, post office.

Interesting words
stationery   prescription   toiletries

Activities
Visit:	many shops
	a shopping centre: count number of types of shops, e.g. three chemists, two supermarkets, and so on
	Study local shops closely; learn their names.
Songs:	Tall shops in the town
	Rub-a-dub-dub
	Pat-a-cake, pat-a-cake, baker's man
Movement/drama:	mime going shopping
Cookery:	buy items from various shops for cookery − make a cookery book

Art work
Cut out large magazine pictures of fruit and vegetables. Paste on to big sheet of paper – label it 'The greengrocer sells these', and make similar pictures of the other shops.
Make charts to illustrate either the number of shops visited or what each shop sells.

Sport

Points for discussion
Probably the only sports the mentally handicapped child comes in contact with are those on TV, for example:

Sports with a ball	*Without a ball*
football	boxing
rugby	wrestling
cricket	show jumping
tennis	horse racing
snooker	motor racing
	athletics

Names associated with sports: Wembley, Olympics, Ascot, Grand National, Derby.
Winter sports: ski-ing, skating, bobsleigh.

Interesting words

gymnast	prize	racket
steeplechase	winner	bat
stadium		

Activities
Visits:	look in a sports-shop window
	a sports centre, swimming pool, ice rink
	an (empty) football or cricket ground
Song:	I can do anything better than you!
Movement/drama:	dribble ball, jump, run, chase – also in slow motion (action replay!)

Art work
Ideal for following up topical subjects.
Make a simple model racetrack with lasagne (soften it in boiling water

to bend it slightly). Make stadium seats with tiered matchboxes glued together.

Cut out Sunday colour-supplement magazine pictures of Olympics and make collage.

Child could make his own picture of his favourite sport.

Spring
(see also Chapter 5: Nature; Flowers)

Points for discussion
    new growth after cold winter
    warmer weather
    trees budding (horse chestnut very interesting – sticky bud becomes furry)
    hibernating animals start to awake
    tadpoles begin to appear in ponds
    blossom appears on trees (pink almond is the first)
    pussy-willow catkins on trees
    birds singing – especially the cuckoo
    spring flowers: snowdrop, daffodil, tulip, crocus

Interesting words
    shoots   blooming

Activities
Visits: garden centres
          parks and gardens
          look at private gardens
Songs: Chick, chick, chick, chick chicken ... lay a little egg for me
          Here we go gathering nuts in May
          Mary, Mary, quite contrary
Poem: Der Spring has sprung
Hang out wool, feathers, moss, grass, cotton, etc. Notice what the birds take first.

Art work
Many young, fluffy, furry animals are suitable for a spring collage: ducklings, lambs, chickens, bunnies, foals, calves.

Make a tree in blossom by winding pink crêpe paper around bare twigs – stand in a vase or hang as a mobile.

Summer

Points for discussion

holidays	sun oil (cream)	ice-cream
sand	stops sunburn	caterpillars
seaside	deck-chair	summer sounds (see
seaweed	strawberries and	Music, page 93)
shells	cream	cricket
sunglasses	butterflies	tennis
sunbathing	bees (honey)	

summer flowers: roses, sunflowers, nasturtiums

Interesting words

vacation	holidaymaker	travel agent
abroad	tourist	surf

Activities

Visits: seaside
             airport (if possible) to see the holidaymaker
Songs: Puffa train
Movement/drama: fluttery butterfly
             busy bee
             nodding flowers
             calm sea, small waves, choppy sea, very rough sea
             mime building sandcastles

Art work

Make a paper butterfly attached to string on a stick.

Make a giant ice-cream: use cornflakes for the cone and cotton-wool for the ice, pale-coloured tissue-paper for the different flavours of ice.

Make a giant sunflower: huge petals of orange or yellow cellophane and a centre of small, dark brown scraps of cloth on a long, green, leafy stem. (Could be painted or made of hand prints.)

Make a large, furry caterpillar on a green leaf.

Make a seaside collage.

Toys

Activities

Visit: toyshop; toymaker, if possible

Songs: I know a teddy bear
Teddy bears' picnic
Miss Polly had a dolly

Movement/drama: pop-up jack-in-a-box
stiff puppet or toy soldier
rag doll
rocking horse
bricks, building up — falling down

Art work

Make a rag doll. Make a peg doll, out of a dolly peg.
Make a collage of a toyshop, soldier, train, teddy bear and a doll.

Transport
(see also Flying; Water)

Points for discussion

Road	*Water*	*Air*
lorry	ship	aeroplane
car	boat	helicopter
van	barge	glider
wagon	yacht	balloon
coach	ferry	
bus	submarine	*Overland*
taxi	hovercraft	tank
bicycle	hydrofoil	tractor
horse and carriage	canoe	pram
fire engine	tanker	pushchair
ambulance	*Rail*	trolley
police car	train	handcart
	underground	wheelbarrow

Interesting words

fly	guide	paddle
ride	steer	cabin
drive	travel	navigator
pilot	passenger	navigation
captain	coast	timetable
pedal	cruise	juggernaut

Activities

Visits: go for a ride on a bus; in a train
visit the airport and docks, if possible the seaside, a marina or canal

Songs: Puffa train
Row your boat
Morningtown ride

Movement/drama: like a train, shunting back and forth
in pairs, row boats
bobbing on water, like a boat
glide like a glider
ride a bike
push a wheelbarrow

Art work

Air transport makes a good mobile.
Free painting – child paints a picture of his dad's car.
Make 3-D model of train (see Handicrafts – wood).
Use cartons as cars, lorries, etc. to play in. Paint them.

Trees

Points for discussion

tall	natural (forest)
small	planted (orchard)
old	plantation – trees planted by
new	Forestry Commission

Count the rings in trunk for age. Some trees lose leaves, some are evergreen. Autumn colour.

Easy to recognize:
poplar — tall, thin, straight (branches parallel to trunk)
silver birch — silvery bark, small tree
oak — large tree, distinctive leaf (many rounded knobs)
holly — shiny, prickly leaf, some berries

Some trees have:	*Some trees have blossom*:
acorns (oak)	cherry
pine-cones (pine)	almond
fir-cones (fir)	apple
catkins (willow, hazel)	pear
conkers (horse chestnut)	peach
fruit (apple, pear, etc.)	
berries (holly, mountain ash)	

Interesting words
   evergreen   copse   dell   glade

Activities

Visits:	woodland
	forests
	orchards
	nature trail
	parkland
	collect twigs and leaves
Songs:	I had a little nut tree
	Here we go round the mulberry bush
	Blowin' in the wind
Movement/drama:	tall stately poplar, swaying at top only
	large oak tree, all branches moving
	forest, all moving together in the wind
	starting with slight breeze, build up to stormy weather, lightning strikes one or two trees

Art work
Collect twigs and pine-cones, paint white, tie together with black cotton, so that pine-cones dangle beneath twigs.
Hang decorated cones in front of black paper for effective winter mobile.
Make leaf prints.
Take bark rubbings.
Cornflakes make effective Autumn leaves for collage work.

Vegetables
(see also Chapter 4: Cookery)

Points for discussion

Fresh	*Tinned*	*Dried*
Eat raw (then cooked)	baked beans	butter beans
white cabbage	peas	kidney beans
potato	carrots	haricot beans
onion	butter beans	onions
carrot		mixed vegetables
peas	*Frozen*	peas
cauliflower	mixed vegetables	
green beans	peas	
Salad vegetables	sprouts	
lettuce	cauliflower	
cucumber	carrots	
radish	chips	
Only eat cooked (add salt)		
spring cabbage		
sprouts		
turnip		
swede } mix with carrots		
parsnip		

Interesting words

crisp	raw	slice
crunchy	good health	chop
sweet	peel	preserve
tender	scrape	

Activities
Visit: greengrocer's, supermarket, market
Purchase goods for cookery.

Art work
Make potato prints; carrot prints. Half an onion makes an attractive print too.
Cut out pictures of vegetables.
Make mosaics: tiny scraps of material glued in one large picture of a vegetable.

Visits

Here is a list of visits which should be suitable. They will depend, however, on where the school is situated.

Places of interest
museum
art gallery
church
cathedral
ten-pin bowling
   alley
ice rink
theatre
sports centre
nature trails
forest
woodland
hilly country
moorland
parkland
large country
   house
cafe

Animals
pets' corner
farm
pet shop
zoo
police stables
safari park
police dogs
kennels
marineland

Travel
bus depot
tram depot
railway station
airport
tramway
   museum
railway museum
boat trip
ferry trip
underground
   trip
bus journey
train journey
carriage
   museum

Watery visits
seaside
lakeland
stream
river
pond
canal
reservoir
sewage farm

Water

(see also Chapter 5: Nature; Fish; Transport)

Points for discussion

In water	*On water*	*Water itself*
fish	ship	rain
whale	boat	raindrops
shark	yacht	lake
dolphin	duck	river
turtle	swan	pond
octopus	lighthouse	canal
jellyfish	oil rig	sea
frogmen	seaplane	puddle
submarine	water-ski	stream
		in a tap
		drink it
		wash with it
		flowers and plants need it
		cook with it

Interesting words

bubbles	plunge	meander
oxygen	depth	gush
undersea	breathe	drip
submerge	flow	burst

Activities

Visits:	marineland
	seaside
	fishmonger's shop
	canal (lock gates)
	lake, pond, stream or river
Songs:	All the ducks are swimming on the water
	There's a tiny house, by a tiny stream
Movement/drama:	diver, fish, octopus, submarine, dolphin, turtle
	the sea — calm, then gradually becoming a raging torrent
	mime making a drink, having a drink

Art work
Blue cellophane is very effective covering a large collage of the sea.
Make an octopus from a cotton-reel and four pipe cleaners.
Green prints are attractive for a turtle.
Build an oil rig with matchboxes and cocktail sticks, set in blue
  Polyfilla (make the plaster blue by adding blue powder-paint to the
  dry powder before mixing with water). Bubbles can be represented
  by blue circles.

Weather

Points for discussion

hot	misty	frosty
cold	foggy	snowing
sunny	wet	stormy
cloudy	raining	blizzard
umbrella	damp	warm
sunshade	windy	cool
rainbow		

Seasonal weather: Summer, Winter, Spring, Autumn.
Suitable clothes appropriate to weather.

Interesting words

breezy	cloudburst	barometer
blustery	weather-cock	thermometer
squall	weather-vane	temperature
gale	raining cats and dogs	

Activities

Rhymes:	It's raining, it's pouring
	Whether the weather be fine
Songs:	Zip-a-dee-do-dah
	Blowin' in the wind
	Raindrops are falling on my head
	I can sing a rainbow
Movement/drama:	shivering and shaking
	waking up cold in winter
	running in the rain
	playing in the snow

Art work

The older class could make a weather chart themselves for the classroom. Suitable pictures for a simple weather chart could be cut from magazines, for example:

(a) sunny – picture of person sunbathing, wearing sunglasses; a sunset

(b) raining – watching rain through the window; umbrella; wellington boots

(c) windy – pictures of flags or windmills

(d) clouds – could be cut from calendar pictures

(e) snow – winter-sports picture, e.g. ski-ing

(f) fog – difficult to represent, could possibly use part of a picture of an impressionist painting, or cover bright picture with tracing paper.

(g) cold – picture of child wrapped up.

The teacher could print words in glue above each picture for the child to sprinkle lentils, split peas, rice or barley over, to make the words stand out.

Western
(see also Red Indian)

Points for discussion

cowboys	sheriff	Rocky Mountains
Indians	boots	herd
horses	spurs	drive
saddle	horseshoe	cowhand
stirrup	branding	ranch
covered wagon	buffalo	trail boss
lasso	steer	deputy
Buffalo Bill	camp fire	cattle
robbers	saloon	

Interesting words

prairie	hyena	payroll
grasslands	stampede	posse

Activities

Songs: Take me back to the black hills
        Home on the range
        She'll be comin' round the mountain
        Yankee doodle dandy

Movement/drama: horses' movements
                 stampeding cattle
                 making a camp fire
                 driving a herd
                 holding up the stagecoach
                 catching the robbers

Art work

Make a covered wagon from boxes and clothes-horse to play in.
Cowboy scene, with wagons, camp fire, cowboys – good as a silhouette.
Make a large covered wagon, collage – very decorative.

Winter

Points for discussion

    some animals hibernate
    cold weather – some animals keep warm with fur
    frost, ice and snow
    evergreen trees; catkins on hazel tree
    holly; mistletoe
    Christmas festivities
    coal fires to keep warm
    fur coats; warm clothing
    Eskimos always have winter
    polar bears keep warm with white fur, which doesn't show against the snow
    feed the birds – they can't get food from hard, frosty ground
    dark early: lights on; heating on

Interesting words

Arctic	nippy	igloo
polar	icicles	perish
ice-cap		

Activities

Bring ice into classroom, draw round it, watch it melt and shrink.

Song: Here we go round the mulberry bush

Movement: shivering, teeth chattering, shaking

mime wrapping up warm: boots, hat, coat, scarf, mittens

Art work

Make an Eskimo scene. Igloo from potato prints (white on black or blue paper). Polar bear upright or horizontal.

Make a silhouette scene (white shapes on black paper) to represent snow. Tapering trees, squares for houses and rounded snowmen.

Paint twigs white, push into *Polyfilla*, add a plastic robin, deer or snowman, tin-foil pond, some pine-cones and stones, to make a simple wintry scene.

Wood
(see also Handicrafts: wood)

Points for discussion

table	bookcase	many toy bricks
chair	door	climbing frame
wardrobe	window-sill	pencil
desk	window-frame	TV surround
clogs	cupboard	fence, gate

Interesting words

polishing	wood finish	creosote
shining	sawdust	woodworm
veneer		

Activities

Visits: timber yard, if possible; building site

Rhyme: Tell me little woodworm (Spike Milligan)

Art work

Use wood shavings for hair, lion's mane, etc.

Polished wood makes an attractive base for pictures.

Hammer nails into wood.

Paint wood (mix paint with PVA glue for easier coverage).

Make abstract design on wood with nails, screws, nuts and bolts, etc.

Glue offcuts together to make models or abstract shapes (use *Evo-Stik*).

Zoo
(see also Animals)

Points for discussion
Wild animals in cages. Open air kinder (e.g. safari park).

elephant	lion	leopard
giraffe	zebra	rhinoceros
kangaroo	monkey	crocodile
tiger	hippopotamus	donkey
alligator	bat	gorilla
sloth	deer	parrot
seal	sea-lion	wolf

Interesting words

monkey house   reptile house   aquarium   zookeeper

Activities

Visit: zoo, safari park, circus: which is kindest for the animals?
Songs: Nelly the elephant
                   The elephant goes like this and that
                   We're all going to the zoo tomorrow
Movement/drama: elephant – slow, heavy
                   lion pacing in cage
                   monkey climbing
                   kangaroo jumping

Art work
(see also Animals)
Put animal pictures in boxes; make bars in front.
Make pictures of funny animals – mixed-up legs, head and body.

Further ideas for themes

fairground	South Seas	drinks
Mexico	monsters	wheels
circus	food	Holland

Bibliography

DENHAM, S. and K. (1969) *Pets for Children* Hamlyn All-Colour Paperbacks

FINNIE, Nancy R. (1974, 2nd edition) *Handling the Young Cerebral Palsied Child at Home* Heinemann

GILBERT, J. (1976) *Musical Activities with Young Children* Ward Lock Educational

Golden Hands Series (1976) *Golden Hands Encyclopedia of Crafts* Marshall Cavendish

HARROP, Beatrice (ed) (1975) *Apusskido: Songs for Children* A. & C. Black

LAW, Felicia (1971) *Something to Make* Penguin

MANDELL, M. and WOOD, R. (1970) *Make Your Own Musical Instruments* Bailey Bros

MATTERSON, Elizabeth (1969) *This Little Puffin* Puffin Books

MILLIGAN, Spike (1968) *Silly Verse for Kids* Puffin Books

RUSSELL, Joan (1965) *Creative Dance in the Primary School* Macdonald & Evans

SCHOOLS COUNCIL (1967) *Mathematics Begins* (Nuffield Mathematics Project) W. & R. Chambers and John Murray

SHERIDAN, Mary (1968) *Developmental Progress of Infants and Young Children (Department of Health Report)* HMSO

SOPER, Tony (1975) *The New Bird Table Book* Pan

STEVENS, Mildred (1976) *The Educational and Social Needs of Children with Severe Handicap* Arnold

STEVENS, Mildred (1978) *Observe – Then Teach* Arnold

An additional book which teachers should recommend to all parents:

STONE, Judith and TAYLOR, Felicity (1977) *A Handbook for Parents with a Handicapped Child* Arrow Books

Index